The Standards-Based Digital School Leader Portfolio

A Handbook for Preparation and Practice

Gregory M. Hauser
Dennis W. Koutouzos

Rowman & Littlefield Education
Lanham, Maryland • Toronto • Oxford
2005

Published in the United States of America
by Rowman & Littlefield Education
A Division of Rowman & Littlefield Publishers, Inc.
A wholly owned subsidiary of The Rowman & Littlefield Publishing Group, Inc.
4501 Forbes Boulevard, Suite 200, Lanham, Maryland 20706
www.rowmaneducation.com

PO Box 317
Oxford
OX2 9RU, UK

Copyright © 2005 Gregory M. Hauser and Dennis W. Koutouzos

All rights reserved. No part of this publication may be reproduced, stored in a retrieval system, or transmitted in any form or by any means, electronic, mechanical, photocopying, recording, or otherwise, without the prior permission of the publisher.

British Library Cataloguing in Publication Information Available

Library of Congress Cataloging-in-Publication Data

Hauser, Gregory M., 1953–
  The standards-based digital school leader portfolio : a handbook for preparation and practice / Gregory M. Hauser, Dennis W. Koutouzos.
    p. cm.
  Includes bibliographical references.
  ISBN 1-57886-271-X (pbk. : alk. paper)
  1. Portfolios in education—Computer-aided design—Handbooks, manuals, etc. 2. School administrators—United States—Handbooks, manuals, etc.
I. Koutouzos, Dennis W., 1941– . II. Title.
LB1029.P67H38 2005
371.2′011—dc22
                                                                    2005009611

∞ ™ The paper used in this publication meets the minimum requirements of American National Standard for Information Sciences—Permanence of Paper for Printed Library Materials, ANSI/NISO Z39.48–1992. Manufactured in the United States of America.

Contents

Acknowledgments		v
Introduction		vii
1	History and Development of the Standards-Based Digital School Leader Portfolio	1
2	The Development of the Standards-Based Digital Portfolio	15
3	Digital Format Options	51
4	The PowerPoint Option	63
5	The TaskStream Option	69
6	Evaluation of the Standards-Based Digital Portfolio	83
Appendix A: ISLLC Self-Assessment		89
Appendix B: TSSA Self-Assessment		107
Appendix C: ISLLC Standards Planner		113
Appendix D: TSSA Standards Planner		125
Appendix E: Formative Evaluation Rubric		129
Appendix F: Summative Rubric		131
References		133
About the Authors		141

Acknowledgments

This text was the result of the generous assistance of numerous colleagues. In particular, I would like to especially thank Dennis Koutouzos for his many contributions. He not only authored chapter 3 but helped in virtually every aspect of this project including editing numerous drafts of each chapter and sharing his considerable expertise in educational technology. This text is as much a reflection of his good work as it is mine. My faculty colleagues at Roosevelt University, Cozette Buckney, Tom Kersten, Jerry Chapman, Tom Thomas, and George Olson provided invaluable editorial assistance to various drafts of the text. Susan Katz, another faculty colleague, provided useful feedback based on her own experiences as well as those of her students in working with the standards-based digital school leader portfolio. I would like to extend my appreciation for the assistance and support from TaskStream including: Aitken Thompson, Chief Operating Officer; Webster Thompson, Executive Vice President; and Seth Giammanco, Director of Client Operations. Anna Krumwiede, my graduate assistant, patiently and cheerfully assisted me along the way providing research support. A note of appreciation is extended to the Spencer Foundation for their financial support. It is important to mention Richard White, a technology consultant, who served as a reviewer of the text proposal. Finally, I would like to thank the many classes of master's and doctoral students who provided feedback to various versions of the standards-based digital school leader portfolio template.

Introduction

While there are an increasing number of resource handbooks available to assist educators in the development of digital portfolios, very few are devoted exclusively to school leaders. In response to this critical void in the literature, we have created this practitioner handbook to assist school leaders, educational leaders, and school leader candidates in developing and using standards-based digital school portfolios.

A number of issues associated with the design and use of a standards-based digital portfolio warrant consideration by educational leadership faculty. Deciding how to incorporate a standards-based digital school leader portfolio into the curriculum requires that you consider four major factors: hardware, software, faculty, and pedagogy. The hardware issues involve establishing standards to ensure that those who need to access the digital portfolio can access it with the least amount of difficulty. Educational leaders are advised to establish hardware configurations so school leader candidates can create digital portfolios. Often this decision is easier if the institution has already established hardware and software standards. If hardware and software standards are not clearly established, educational leaders and school leader candidates will likely experience hardware and software incompatibility issues. One possible strategy to address this issue is to use the same hardware and software standards as one of the college's or university's computer laboratories. In this way, school leader candidates can access the designated hardware and software configuration without additional cost. Make sure to carefully consider the training needs of educational leaders using the software and hardware described in this book, however. Educational leaders who extensively use technology in their courses will likely experience little difficulty in incorporating the standards-based digital school leader portfolio described in this book. Other educational leaders will likely need training. Another benefit of using hardware and software standards that are consistent with the college or university standards is that most colleges and universities today have full-time computer technicians to provide training and assistance. Using supported hardware and software will also ensure that educational leaders needing training or assistance will have access to in-house trainers.

The templates and samples in this book could provide a useful framework for training educational leaders. A special concern relates to the training of adjunct educational leaders. Unless adjunct faculty members teach regularly in the program, they might not be as proficient as their full-time colleagues in using the hardware and software to develop the digital portfolio. If the standards-based digital school leader portfolio is implemented across the curriculum, these staff training issues become more complicated given the number of faculty members. On the other hand, the faculty training issues can be minimized by incorporating the standards-based digital school leader portfolio into the practicum sequence, thus requiring that only the faculty members who teach these courses be trained.

There are three primary ways educational leaders can incorporate the standards-based digital school leader portfolio into their curriculum. First, they can use it in each course across the curriculum. Second, educational leaders can use it in the practicums to document school leader candidate work in the field. The educational leaders at Roosevelt University used this particular approach to test the standards-based digital school leader portfolio template with a few faculty members and students (Hauser & Katz, 2004). The knowledge and experience they gained guided them when implementing the digital portfolio across their curriculum. Third, educational leaders can use the digital portfolio as an alternative to the comprehensive examination in educational leadership programs.

There are many pedagogical benefits to educational leaders and school leader candidates when they use the standards-based digital school leader portfolios. The digital portfolio process will stimulate faculty members' thinking in a number of ways. First, faculty members can exercise greater flexibility and creativity when designing course assignments. Both faculty members and students might view assignments differently when assignments have the potential to become part of a portfolio. Faculty members might reassess individual courses and the total curriculum in light of this approach to authentic assessment. Also, the digital format could stimulate faculty members' creativity with the delivery of content and in course assignments. Second, the portfolio process will encourage educational leaders to ensure that courses provide experiential projects, activities, and artifacts appropriate for the development of a portfolio. Third, research suggests that portfolio assessment could increase faculty-student communication as well as change the content of that communication if reflection and feedback is used in the portfolio process (Cole & Struyk, 1997). Fourth, if the portfolio is used across the curriculum, faculty members can anticipate having a richer and fuller insight into how each course and the entire curriculum prepares school leader candidates to meet professional standards. The portfolio process could thus become an element of program evaluation. Fifth, faculty members involved in distance learning could discover the convenience of the portfolio process in digital format over the conventional paper format (Mills, 1997). Sixth, faculty members will develop higher-level technology skills. Educational leaders who have used digital portfolios in their curriculum comment favorably regarding their own proficiency using various hardware and software. Finally, there is an acute need for educational leaders to better prepare school leaders for their responsibilities associated with technology. Unfortunately, many educational leadership curricula are lacking in this area. "Looking closely at principal preparation programs at our universities, the role of the principal as technology leader is only mentioned in passing" (Creighton, 2003, p. 3). Faculty members can use the digital portfolio as a powerful tool to systematically infuse technology into the curriculum.

The benefits to school leader candidates of developing digital portfolios are numerous. Some of the benefits of the portfolio process to teachers are also applicable to school leader candidates. These include self-assessment and reflection (Barton & Collins, 1993), personal satisfaction and renewal (Cushman, 1999), empowerment, collaboration (Constantino & De Lorenzo, 2002), and holistic assessment (Barton & Collins, 1993; Hunter, 1998). In addition, specific benefits have been identified for school leader candidates. For example, Yerkes & Guaglianone (1998) note that "often begun as part of graduate coursework, the administrative portfolio can be used to self-evaluate, monitor professional growth and development, document specific competencies, or prepare for a job interview" (p. 28). Including the standards-based digital portfolio in the educational leadership curriculum could help school leader candidates model and use portfolio assessment and technology when they become school leaders. These benefits are critical because "aspiring principals must become proficient in developing and applying technology skills, such as designing websites and electronic portfolios, and participating in video conferencing" (Chirichello, 2001, p. 47). In particular, demonstrating their ability to use a complex array of hardware and software applications is a potent benefit to school leader candidates. Also, the standards-based digital portfolio allows school leader candidates to apply this form of authentic assessment.

These aforementioned benefits to educational leaders and school leader candidates are essential for many practitioners. According to Kilbane and Milman (2003), "Two knowledge areas in which many principals require development are technology and authentic assessment. The creation of a portfolio in digital format provides principals [with] a much-needed venue for developing knowledge and skills in these areas" (p. 147). With regard to technology, school leaders must become technology activists. "Education administrators must vision, facilitate, model and embrace technology" (Metropolitan Planning Council, 2002, p. 22). In particular, "there is a dynamic shift occurring in this country as we move from traditional definitions of learning and course design to models of engaged learning that involve more student interaction, more connections among students, more involvement of teachers as facilitators, and more emphasis on technology as a tool for learning" (Jones et al., 1999, p. 2). This same report also recognizes a core problem in the effective use of technology in schools by noting that "it is not enough to provide the technology and connections so that all educators can participate in making decisions about learning and technology; rather, it is vital to provide ongoing professional development so that all educators will participate" (Jones et al., 1999, p. 332). As to the knowledge of authentic assessment, portfolio use by school leaders facilitates leadership effectiveness, enhances student achievement and the professional development of teachers, and encourages collaboration and communication (Marcoux et al., 2003). Portfolios are also useful to school leaders "as evidence of improvement, as [an] organizer [and a] record of achievement, [and as a] collection of work samples" (Wildy & Wallace, 1998, p. 126). Thus, just as the digital portfolio process benefits educational leaders and school leader candidates, it is also a tool for using technology and authentic assessment, while providing personal and professional benefits to school leaders.

However, there are challenges to using the standards-based digital portfolios. Given the paucity of research on digital portfolios, we extrapolate some of these challenges from general literature on the portfolio process. In general, there are five major challenges to developing digital portfolios. First, using digital portfolios in the curriculum requires extensive and careful planning (Wright, Stallworth, & Ray, 2002). Second, creating a portfolio is labor-intensive (Constantino & De Lorenzo, 2002; Wheeler, 1993). A third challenge is that it is time-consuming (Wright, Stallworth, & Ray, 2002; Wheeler, 1993). Fourth, evaluating the portfolio is complicated because of the variety of possible artifacts. "The more diverse the documentation, the more difficult it becomes to compare and evaluate the portfolio" (Constantino & De Lorenzo, 2002, p. 7). Fifth, the complex and changing nature of hardware and software requires additional commitment of human and capital resources.

In addition to these more general challenges, Wildy and Wallace (1998) conducted a study of school leaders that use the portfolio process for accountability and identified tensions "between theory and practice; between public and private demands of portfolios; between the practical nature of leaders' work and the reflective nature of the portfolio; between the portfolio as product and as process; [and] between choice and compliance" (p. 123).

There is no set of strategies to address all of these challenges in every educational setting. Connecting theory and practice, while not the result of using a digital portfolio, could occur when a digital portfolio is required. Because the digital portfolio is easily shared with colleagues, it lends itself to collaboration. At the same time, reflection is also a personal endeavor. Thus, there is a tension between the public nature of a digital portfolio and the private reflection of its creator. With regard to the tension between the practical nature of school leader's work and reflection, Wildy and Wallace (1998) found that "the inquiring, self-critical, analytical and reflective processes of a portfolio culture are also at odds with the school expectations of leaders to be decisive, confident and authoritative" (p. 11). Whether a digital portfolio is a product, a process, or both is a challenge that educational leaders and school leader candidates need to carefully explore. The interesting tension between choice and compliance is directly related to developing this book. Educational leaders should carefully consider how many guidelines they provide for constructing a digital portfolio and how much choice they give school leader candidates in the structure and content of the digital portfolio. We recommend a balance between these two. Also, establishing clear hardware and software standards eases access and reduces the amount of training needed. Typically, educational leaders who use portfolios provide an outline for the content of the digital portfolio (Chirichello, 2001; Hauser & Katz, 2004; Meadows, Dyal, & Wright, 1998; Testerman & Hall, 2001; Wildy & Wallace, 1998; Yerkes, 1995).

The educational leaders and school leader candidates at Roosevelt University identified the following strategies for meeting these challenges (Hauser & Katz, 2004). First, provide sufficient time, technology training, and other resources to faculty members in order to successfully incorporate the digital portfolio into the curriculum. Second, pilot the standards-based digital portfolio process in one or more courses and expand to the entire curriculum over time. Third, provide templates and tools for school leader candidates to choose from when developing digital portfolios. Fourth, provide partially completed examples of digital portfolios to stimulate student creativity. Fifth, provide ample computer laboratory time. Sixth, use lower-level technology software and hardware initially and incorporate more sophisticated technology as training and skill level warrant.

ORGANIZATION OF THE BOOK

This book is designed as a handbook for educational leaders and school leader candidates. It can be used as a primary or supplemental text in the educational leadership curriculum or for staff development training. The two different templates, TaskStream and PowerPoint, are consistent with our view that there is no single "best way" to develop a standards-base digital school leader portfolio. The book is organized as follows:

- Chapter 1 provides a brief history of the development and use of standards-based digital portfolios.

- Chapter 2 details a suggested outline and design of the digital portfolio.
- Chapter 3 provides an overview of various digital options and criteria for selecting options.
- Chapter 4 details a suggested outline and design of the digital portfolio using PowerPoint.
- Chapter 5 details a suggested outline and design of the digital portfolio using TaskStream.
- Chapter 6 addresses the presentation or evaluation of the standards-based digital portfolio.

A summary is included at the end of each chapter. Appendixes provide samples for planning and building the portfolio and linking to leadership standards.

Chapter One

History and Development of the Standards-Based Digital School Leader Portfolio

This chapter explores essential questions related to digital school leadership portfolios: What is a standards-based digital portfolio? Who uses them? How are they used? Why are they used? It also offers background on the characteristics, purposes, uses, and audiences for a standards-based digital portfolio. We begin by discussing how the school leader or candidate can individualize the digital school leader portfolio to accommodate her professional interests and needs.

WHAT IS A STANDARDS-BASED DIGITAL PORTFOLIO?

The term "standards-based digital portfolio" is a complicated concept best understood by examining its parts. The qualifiers "digital" and "standards-based" help place "portfolio" in context.

We shall begin by exploring the term "portfolio." It might be a surprise to know just how widely they are used today. Although portfolios were initially used in the visual arts (Castiglione, 1996), they have more recently been adapted to a host of diverse academic disciplines from medicine (Snadden & Thomas, 1998; Mathers et al., 1999) to library science (Snavely & Wright, 2003). Interest in portfolios in modern American society is evident by their use at local (Richard, 2001), state (Berryman,

2001), national (Crisp & Leggett, 1995), and international levels (Maeroff, 1991).

Since the early 1990s, there has been a growing body of literature on using portfolios in teacher education (Constantino & De Lorenzo, 1998, 2002; Rieman, 2000), counselor education (Baltimore et al., 1996), and school leadership (Brown & Irby, 2001; Deitz, 2001; Nicholson, 2004). Portfolios have only been widely used in higher education (Fisher, 1993), particularly in schools, colleges, and departments of education, since the 1990s (Barton & Collins, 1993).

Educational professionals began using portfolios because of the concept of authentic assessment (Wiggins, 1989). Authentic assessment is sometimes termed as authentic intellectual achievement, which has three characteristics, namely, "construction of knowledge, disciplined inquiry, and value beyond school" (Newmann, Marks, & Gamoran, 1996, p. 282). Constructing knowledge requires production rather than a restatement of information. Disciplined inquiry integrates prior knowledge, develops an in-depth understanding of a problem or relationship, and requires elaborate communication of findings. The third criterion, value beyond school, means applying learning to life experiences. Assessment refers to learning theory and practice beyond the narrow traditional forms of psychological testing and measurement (Cumming & Maxwell, 1999). A portfolio, in the context of this book, is an authentic assessment tool used by school leaders and school leader candidates to demonstrate intellectual accomplishment. The criteria for assessing the portfolio—construction of knowledge, disciplined inquiry, and value beyond school—are in the context of professional standards.

As a tool to document intellectual accomplishment, the portfolio is substantively guided by professional standards, thus the qualifier "standards-based." This emphasis on standards in particular, and testing and measurement in general, is an outgrowth of the current wave of school reform. This reform movement began with the publication of *A Nation at Risk: The Imperative for Educational Reform* (National Commission for Excellence in Education, 1983). Since the early 1990s, state and national standards and their purported objective outcomes have been viewed as the principal means to assess student achievement, teacher competence, and school leader quality. In regard to school leadership, "implementing the No Child Left Behind Act (NCLB) of 2001 is forcing us to confront the weaknesses of contemporary school leadership and is making it impossible to ignore the escalating need for higher quality principals—individuals who have been prepared to provide the instructional leadership necessary to improve student achievement" (Hale & Moorman, 2003, p. 1). The portfolio has promise as a way for school leaders to respond to these trends (Ediger, 2001).

One of the most important events for national professional standards occurred in 1994 when the National Policy Board for Educational Administration (NPBEA) formed the Interstate School Leader Licensure Consortium (ISLLC) to develop school leader standards (Murphy, 2003). The NPBEA is an association of ten organizations interested in school leadership, including the National Council for the Accreditation of Teachers (NCATE), the University Council for Educational Administration (UCEA), the American Association of Colleges of Teacher Education (AACTE), and others. When created by the NPBEA, the ISLLC included twenty-four member states as well as other organizations interested in school leadership.

The six ISLLC standards were published in 1996 and state that a school administrator is an educational leader who promotes the success of all students by

1. facilitating the development, articulation, implementation, and stewardship of a vision of learning that is shared and supported by the community;
2. advocating, nurturing, and sustaining a school culture and instructional program conducive to student learning and staff professional growth;
3. ensuring management of the organization, operations, and resources for a safe, efficient, and effective learning environment;
4. collaborating with families and community members, responding to diverse community interests and needs, and mobilizing community resources;
5. acting with integrity, fairness, and in an ethical manner; and
6. understanding, responding to, and influencing the larger political, social, economic, legal, and cultural context (Council of Chief State School Officers, 1996).

There are three dimensions or elements to each standard: knowledge, dispositions, and performances. Resources are available that provide exemplary projects and artifacts related to these dimensions for each standard (Hackmann, Schmitt-Oliver, & Tracy, 2002). Descriptions of these projects and activities can be incorporated into the digital portfolio.

More recently, there has been concern about the extent to which the NCATE standards were aligned to the ISLLC standards. As a result, the NPBEA developed the Advanced Standards for Educational Leadership for Principals, Superintendents, Curriculum Directors, and Supervisors (National Policy Board for Educational Administration, 2002). The Educational Leadership Constituent Council (ELCC), a consortium of national school leadership organizations, works with higher education school leadership preparation programs seeking NCATE approval using the NPBEA standards (Educational Leadership Constituent Council, 2004; National Council for Accreditation of Teacher Education, 2004).

Lately, the Technology Standards for School Administrators (TSSA) Collaborative developed another important set of standards for school leaders (TSSA Collaborative, 2001). The TSSA Collaborative is comprised of leading national and international school leadership and technology associations including the American Association of School Administrators (AASA), the National School Boards Association (NSBA), the National Association of Elementary School Principals (NAESP), the National Association of Secondary School Principals (NASSP), the Association of Education Service Agencies (AESA), and the International Society for Technology in Education (ISTE), among others. The primary goal of the Collaborative was to develop national standards for what school administrators "should know and be able to do to optimize the effective use of technology" (TSSA Collaborative, 2001). The six TSSA standards are as follows:

1. Leadership and Vision: Educational leaders inspire a shared vision for comprehensive integration of technology and foster an environment and culture conducive to the realization of that vision.
2. Learning and Teaching: Educational leaders ensure that curricular design, instructional strategies, and learning environments integrate appropriate technologies to maximize learning and teaching.
3. Productivity and Professional Practice: Educational leaders apply

technology to enhance their professional practice and to increase their own productivity and that of others.
4. Support, Management, and Operations: Educational leaders ensure the integration of technology to support productive systems for learning and administration.
5. Assessment and Evaluation: Educational leaders use technology to plan and implement comprehensive systems of effective assessment and evaluation.
6. Social, Legal, and Ethical Issues: Educational leaders understand the social, legal, and ethical issues related to technology and model responsible decision making related to these issues. (TSSA Collaborative, 2001)

The content of the standards-based digital school leader portfolio in this book is guided primarily by the six ISLLC standards and the six TSSA standards. Other sets of criteria, such as local, district, and state standards and academic course or program expectations can be added at the discretion of the school leader or school leader candidate.

With a better understanding of the term "standards-based," we now turn to the qualifier "digital." You have likely read about both digital portfolios and electronic portfolios. Are they the same thing? Experts say they are not. As pointed out by Helen Barrett (2004), "an electronic portfolio contains artifacts that may be in analog form, such as a video tape, or may be in computer-readable form; in a digital portfolio, all artifacts have been transformed into computer-readable form." Because this book provides a guide to develop portfolios that are completely in computer-readable form, it uses the term "digital" instead of the more commonly used term, "electronic."

The early 1990s marked an important milestone for how schools use standards-based digital portfolios as an authentic assessment tool with the Exhibitions Project, an initiative by the Coalition for Essential Schools (McDonald, 1996; Niguidula, 1997). "Much more than an electronic file cabinet, digital portfolios are transforming assessment—and becoming a tool for school reform" (Niguidula, 1997, p. 26). As part of the school reform effort, it is imperative that school leaders, trainers, and school leader candidates learn from personal experience how to develop and use standards-based digital portfolios.

WHO USES THEM?

Portfolios have been used by principals and other leadership professionals, trainers, and candidates. Practitioners use portfolios to document professional growth and facilitate career advancement. These practitioners include music educators (Campbell & Brummett, 2002), higher education faculty members (Stanley, 2001), technical writers (Luescher, 2002), and school leaders (Daresh & Playko, 1995; Brown & Irby, 1997, 2001; Yerkes, 1995). Professional trainers use portfolios to evaluate candidate performance in such fields as elementary education (Mick, 1996), secondary education (Cole & Struyk, 1997), school counselor education (Rhyne-Winkler & Wooten, 1996), language and literacy (Davis, 2003), teacher leadership (Bradley, 1995), and special education (Conderman, 2003). Faculty members in school leadership programs are increasingly using portfolio assessments in lieu of comprehensive examinations and to show academic achievement in general (Meadows, Dyal, & Wright, 1998; Meadows & Dyal, 1999). Professional candidates use portfolios to comply with course requirements and advance their careers. In sum, there is growing evidence that educators—especially school leaders and school leader candidates—use portfolios.

HOW ARE THEY USED?

There are several different ways to categorize how portfolios are used depending on who uses them. For example, Wolf and Siu-Runyan (1996) identify three types of portfolios: the ownership portfolio, the feedback portfolio, and the accountability portfolio. The ownership portfolio is used to guide self-directed learning. In this instance, the "how" is guided by personal learning objectives and outcomes. In the feedback portfolio, the leader or leader candidate and a peer coach, collaborator, supervisor, or instructor use the portfolio to collaborate on learning goals and outcomes. The feedback portfolio provides feedback to guide pedagogical practice and professional growth. The accountability portfolio is guided primarily by the district requirements and professional standards or by the instructor to evaluate student achievement. According to Wolf and Siu-Runyan (1996), these different types of student portfolios can be distinguished based on authorship, audience, structure, content, and process.

There are alternative classifications of portfolios. Brown and Irby (2001), for example, describe four different types of portfolios. For our purposes, however, three broad uses for portfolios will be considered, namely, evaluative, developmental, and career. This is consistent with the portfolios described by Wildy and Wallace (1998) and others.

The evaluative portfolio provides a summative evaluation of a school leader's performance or school leader candidate's performance related to various criteria. A school leader might develop an evaluative portfolio in cooperation with a supervisor in response to local, district, state, or the ISLLC standards. To illustrate, in the Chicago Public School system, principals are required to submit a summative evaluation portfolio to their area instructional officer or regional superintendent. There are several other examples of portfolios being used in connection with school leader evaluation (Cruz, 1998; Marcoux, Brown, Irby, & Lara-Alecio, 2003). School leader candidates, working with school leaders, might develop a digital evaluation portfolio to document academic achievement (Meadows, Dyal, & Wright, 1998; Meadows & Dyal, 1999). More specifically, school leader candidates might use digital portfolios to document their achievement of knowledge, performance, and dispositions of the ISLLC standards through digital artifacts for coursework or practical experiences. A key feature of the evaluation portfolio is that it is evaluated externally.

The developmental portfolio can be used to record professional or academic growth. School leaders might use digital portfolios to document their achievement of performance standards associated with continuing professional development units (CPDUs). School leader candidates might develop a digital portfolio to record personal and professional growth as they complete their academic program. Because it is for personal use and not for evaluative use, it is shared with others at the discretion of the creator.

The career portfolio can be used by school leaders or school leader candidates seeking employment or professional advancement (Yerkes, 1995). In this case, school leaders have the opportunity to assemble reflections and artifacts to document their accomplishments far beyond the standard cover letter and resume.

WHY ARE THEY USED?

Barrett (1998, 2004) and Sheingold (1992) identify many advantages for teachers and students who use digital portfolios. These same advantages also apply to school leaders and school leader candidates. Digital portfolios require minimum storage space, in contrast to bulky paper portfolios. This is particularly important for school leaders interested in storing work completed by school leader candidates. It is much easier to create duplicate copies of digital portfolios. Copies are useful for backup and career advancement. Digital portfolios are also more portable than paper portfolios. A digital portfolio stored on diskette, Zip disk, or CD requires very little space, and the Web-based digital portfolio requires no digital space locally. Digital portfolios have a very long shelf life in contrast to paper portfolios, which deteriorate over time. One of the caveats to this long shelf life, however, is changes in software and hardware. The Zip disk is likely to share the same fate as diskettes and Beta videotapes. Consider also some of the difficulties commonly experienced with different versions of Microsoft Office software. The point is that older or obsolete versions of software and hardware can make accessing some artifacts in a digital portfolio difficult. Still, digital portfolios are more accessible than paper portfolios. This is particularly true of the Web-based versions of digital portfolios, accessible through any computer with an Internet connection. The digital portfolio is a potent way for school leaders and school leader candidates to increase their technology skills and model best practices associated with technology. Digital portfolios can be used to facilitate standards-based, learner-centered learning. Using more than one set of professional standards is particularly easy to accomplish with digital portfolios through Web-based digital portfolio tools. Many of the Web-based tools have a standards browsing feature that allows users to choose and interrelate different sets of standards. Kilbane and Milman (2003) summarize, "Digital portfolios help showcase principal's knowledge, leadership, and technology competence, support teaching portfolio initiatives, and teach principals about themselves and their practice" (p. 143).

DEFINITIONS OF PORTFOLIOS IN THE FIELD OF EDUCATION

Given that portfolios are used as an alternative form of authentic assessment in so many subspecialties in education, it is not surprising that there are numerous definitions of portfolios in the literature. These definitions, while seemingly very different, are useful because we can see their commonalities. A portfolio is typically contingent upon "who is creating it," "for whom," and "for what purpose." For example, Arter (1992) offered a general definition of the student portfolio as a "purposeful collection of student work that tells the story of the student's efforts, progress and achievement in a given area" (p. 3). In counselor education programs, potential use of portfolios has been described as follows: "In conjunction with traditional assessment approaches already established, the student counseling portfolio can provide interesting and important documentation for clinical growth and development [and] offer a solution to training problems often encountered by professional counselor programs" (Baltimore et al., 1996). Constantino and De Lorenzo (2002) note a wide range of definitions of portfolios in teacher education literature. "In general, the definitions share many common elements. . . . They consistently affirm the idea that portfolio documentation provides authentic evidence of a teacher's work and is a vehicle for fostering reflection on the art and practice of teaching" (p. 2).

Wolf and Siu-Runyan (1996) identify the following characteristics common to all portfolios. "No matter the particulars of any portfolio system, all portfolios are constructed for clear and sound purposes, contain diverse collections of . . . work and records of progress assembled over time, are framed by reflections and enriched through collaboration, and have as their ultimate aim the advancement of . . . learning" (p. 3).

THE PORTFOLIO CONCEPTUAL MODEL

How do you make sense of all these differences? One way to understand the *who*, *what*, and *how* of a portfolio is to consider three dimensions, namely, the constituency, the content, and the purpose. The constituency refers to *who is using the portfolio*, the content refers to *what is contained in the portfolio*, and the purpose refers to *how the portfolio is used*. See figure 1.1 for a useful graphic representation of these dimensions.

As mentioned previously, digital portfolios, with some editing, can address a combination of constituencies, content, and purposes. The three constituencies under consideration include school leaders, school leader faculty members, and school leader candidates. The content of the portfo-

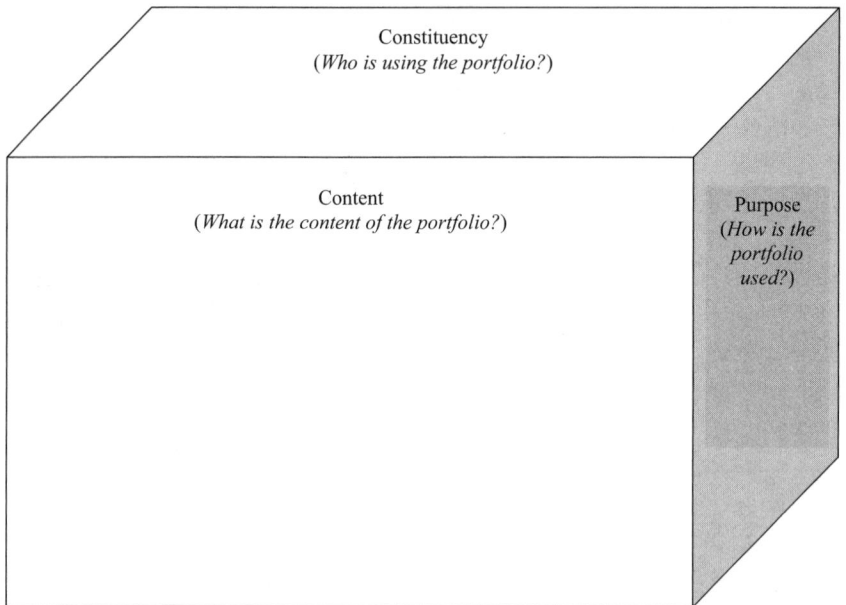

Figure 1.1. Three dimensions of the portfolio

lio addresses local, state, and national standards. The academic program requirements at a university or the criteria of a school district are local standards. State school leadership standards are state standards and the ISLLC standards are national standards. The three purposes for a portfolio are evaluative, developmental, and career. Figure 1.2 shows the possible permutations of constituency, content, and purpose of school leadership digital portfolios.

DEFINITION OF THE STANDARDS-BASED DIGITAL SCHOOL LEADER PORTFOLIO

There are several definitions of the school leader portfolio in the literature. For example, Meadows and Dyal (1999) define the portfolio for school leader candidates as follows: "Leadership portfolios allow aspiring administrators to demonstrate through genuine and practical evidence

History and Development

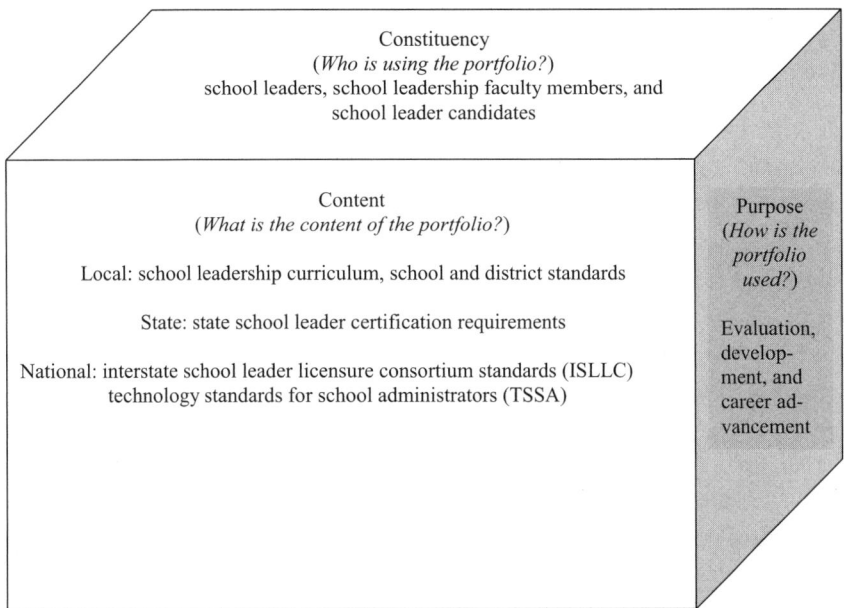

Figure 1.2. Three dimensions of the portfolio related to school leadership preparation and practice

the skills, practices, and strategies essential to becoming successful, competent school leaders."

Brown and Irby (2001) offer the following definition: "The principal portfolio, whether for the purposes of professional or academic growth, evaluation, or career advancement, is a collection of thoughtfully selected exhibits or artifacts and reflections indicative of an individual's experiences and ability to lead and of the individual's progress toward and/or attainment of established goals or criteria" (p. 2). Because our focus is on standards-based content of the portfolio in a digital format, these prior definitions are not sufficient.

With figure 1.2 as a model for the standards-based school leader digital portfolio, refer to the following definition:

> The digital portfolio is used by school leaders, school leadership faculty members, and school leader candidates (*who*) to document the knowledge, performance, and dispositions required by local, state, and national profes-

sional standards (*what*) for evaluative, developmental, and career purposes (*how*).

This inclusive definition, while accommodating the complex differences in constituencies (*who*), content (*what*), and purposes (*how*) as outlined in figure 1.2, is not discrete enough to meet the diverse interests and needs of individuals.

Several possible definitions are provided below to illustrate the differences in constituency, content, and purpose and the *who*, *what*, and *how*. The following is a sample definition of a digital portfolio used by a school leader for professional development:

> The digital portfolio is used by a school leader (*who*) to document the knowledge, performance, and dispositions required by district and state standards (*what*—local and state) as required for continuing professional development (*how*).

A sample definition of a digital portfolio used by a school leader as a tool for career advancement follows:

> The digital portfolio is used by a school leader (*who*) to document the knowledge, performance, and dispositions required by district and state standards (*what*—local and state) for career advancement (*how*).

And here is a sample definition of a digital portfolio used by a school leader for evaluation:

> The digital portfolio is used by a school leader (*who*) to document the knowledge, performance, and dispositions required by district and state standards (*what*—local and state) for the purposes of evaluation (*how*).

The following is a sample definition of a school leader candidate digital portfolio used for evaluation:

> The digital portfolio is used by a school leader candidate (*who*) to document the knowledge, performance, and dispositions required in the internship course (*what*—local) for the purposes of evaluation (*how*).

History and Development 13

And lastly, a sample definition of a school leader candidate digital portfolio used for career advancement follows:

> The digital portfolio is used by a school leader candidate (*who*) to document the knowledge, performance, and dispositions required in the academic program (*what*—local), state (*what*—state), and ISLLC standards (*what*—national) for the purposes of career advancement (*how*).

ACTIVITY

Before attempting to design a digital portfolio, develop one or more working definitions. Construct working definitions of the standards-based digital portfolio by completing figure 1.3. Figure 1.3 also provides space to construct more than one definition if you are planning to create more than one version of the digital portfolio. For example, school leader candidates might wish to create one version of the standards-based digital portfolio to comply with an academic program. At the same time, others might

Constituency	Content	Purpose
Example: *The digital portfolio is used by a school leader*	*to document the knowledge, performance, and dispositions required by local, state, and national standards*	*for the purpose of evaluation*
The digital portfolio is used by . . .	to document the . . .	for the purpose of . . .
(Optional second definition) The digital portfolio is used by . . .	to document the . . .	for the purpose of . . .

Figure 1.3. Definition of my standards-based digital portfolio: completing the sentences

wish to create another version of the digital portfolio for employment purposes. The content and design of each portfolio will be different. Be sure to access the digital file on the accompanying CD, My Definition of the Digital Portfolio, and add it to one or more of the templates.

SUMMARY

On completion of the activity, you should have a working definition of a digital portfolio. The following are additional activities for reflection and portfolio planning:

- Explore the purpose in creating a standards-based digital portfolio with colleagues or other practitioners.
- Consider the implications of using the standards-based digital portfolio as an authentic assessment tool with colleagues or practitioners.
- Compare and contrast the individualized portfolio definition with the definition created by other school leader candidates or other school leaders.
- Create a matrix that identifies how the individualized digital portfolio might compare and contrast with a traditional format.
- Access online library resources to identify articles, monographs, and other digital documents and to enrich understanding of one or more of the topics from this chapter.
- Identify a topic from this chapter on which you would like to read further. Identify online resources to aid in developing the standards-based digital portfolio.

Chapter Two

The Development of the Standards-Based Digital Portfolio

In this chapter we review the outline template for a standards-based digital portfolio and consider linear and nonlinear formats. As a tool for portfolio development, ISLLC and TSSA self-assessments are provided to rate perceived importance and skill level for each standard and to identify priority elements for demonstrating growth. Examples of project-based activities for each standard provide working models. The portfolio self-assessment can be used as a working document to identify objectives, activities, and artifacts for the selected elements of each standard.

WHAT MIGHT BE INCLUDED IN THE OUTLINE?

A personalized definition of the standards-based digital portfolio should be created prior to developing a portfolio outline. Understanding *who is using the portfolio*, *what is the content of the portfolio*, and *how it is being used* guides the creation of one or more definitions. Review the definitions of the standards-based digital portfolio created at the end of chapter 1. The personalized definition guides the development of an outline for the portfolio and is an essential element to review and reflect upon throughout the process.

Developing a general outline is the next step in creating a standards-based digital portfolio. This general outline might include the following sections: (1) personal definition of the standards-based digital portfolio,

(2) professional goal statement, (3) leadership philosophy, (4) ISLLC standards, (5) TSSA standards, and (6) supplemental material. The second section, the professional goal statement, is an opportunity for school leaders to describe their short- and long-term career aspirations. It would be appropriate in this section to include a hyperlink to a current resume. For the leadership philosophy, school leaders or school leader candidates can articulate their own personal leadership philosophy grounded in theory, research, and best practice. In the fourth and fifth sections, school leaders or school leader candidates specify the objectives, activities, and artifacts for ISLLC standards and TSSA standards. Lastly, school leaders or school leader candidates can include supplemental resources not appropriate for any other section of the portfolio. For example, activity time logs could be included here. The internship contract, school or district professional development guidelines, journals, and other artifacts can also be included in this section.

School leaders and school leader candidates should be concerned primarily about two core questions. Does the outline provide the general structure for how I wish to construct the portfolio? Will the outline make sense to the various readers and reviewers who will be examining the portfolio? We strongly encourage modifying and adapting the sample outline in response to these two questions.

SHOULD THE PORTFOLIO BE LINEAR OR NONLINEAR?

Montgomery and Wiley (2004) describe the easiest way to understand the difference between the two as follows: "In that most presentation software is treated as a linear program, the most common use of the programs is to move from one slide to the next, in a specific order" (p. 92). See figure 2.1 for an example of the sample outline in linear format.

A nonlinear format "allows the viewer to 'jump' from slide to slide, or slide to a document outside of the presentation software, and then jump back to the original or to a different slide" (Montgomery & Wiley, 2004, p. 93). This technique is called hyperlinking. By using this technique, "the author can create hyperlinks either by allowing the viewer to click on the words describing where the hyperlink will go (in a manner similar to most website navigation) or by creating a series of 'buttons' that can

Development

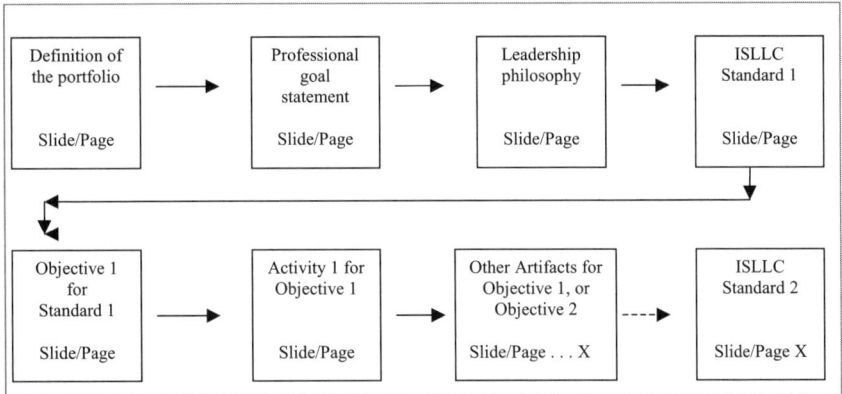

Figure 2.1. Linear standards-based digital portfolio outline in PowerPoint or TaskStream (note that the solid lines display the linear progression from one slide or page to the next)

be 'pushed' by clicking on the button" (Montgomery & Wiley, 2004, p. 93). These hyperlinks allow fluid navigation from slide to slide within the program and to a wide range of artifacts outside of the presentation software. Hyperlinking is typically accomplished using a variety of techniques: "buttons," graphics, text, and Web addresses. The CD accompanying this book provides sample standards-based school leader digital portfolio templates in both PowerPoint and TaskStream. These templates are designed combining features of the linear and nonlinear format and include examples of three different types of hyperlinking. See figure 2.2 for a sample outline that combines linear and nonlinear features. Note that solid lines display linear progression from slide to slide and dotted lines indicate progression chosen by the viewer.

ACTIVITY 1

Consider whether the digital portfolio should be developed in a linear or nonlinear format. The first few slides or pages in which the school leader or school leader candidate introduces herself to the viewer could make most sense in a linear format. On the other hand, formatting the standards section in a linear format could confuse or worse, bore the viewer. Therefore, we recommend that a combination of both linear and nonlinear format options be used in developing the digital portfolio. Because it is

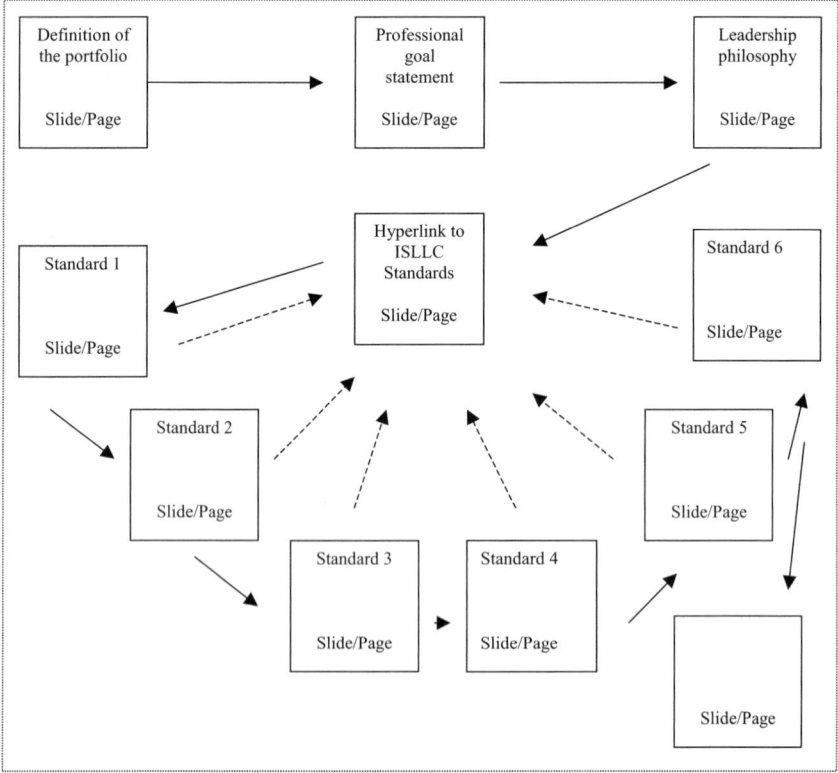

Figure 2.2. Linear and nonlinear standards-based digital portfolio sample outline

difficult to provide guidelines for the extent that a portfolio should be linear versus nonlinear, it is advisable to have critical friends navigate the portfolio. Critical friends can provide valuable feedback on the aforementioned issues. The original format might change during the development of the digital portfolio. Consider the following questions:

- To what extent should the portfolio be linear versus nonlinear?
- What digital portfolio content makes most sense in a linear format?
- What digital portfolio content makes most sense in a nonlinear format?

Complete the ISLLC and the TSSA self-assessments related to perceived importance and beginning skill level for each standard and identify priority areas. The section that contains the professional standards is the most important and complex section of the portfolio. Reflective self-assessment and careful planning are essential in the development of this section. To assist school leaders and school leader candidates with these processes, four instruments that are useful in the planning phase of the digital portfolio are included in this book. Two of these instruments are the ISLLC self-assessment (see appendix A) and the TSSA self-assessment (see appendix B); the other two, the ISLLC standards planner and the TSSA standards planner, are addressed later in this chapter.

The ISLLC self-assessment includes three scales. In the first scale, you rank the relative importance of each element of each standard. In the second scale, you identify your perceived entry skill level. Ranking the relative importance of each element of these standards is important due to the complexity and number of subelements. Not all of these subelements will be perceived as equally important to either school leaders or school leader candidates. Some internal and external factors affecting these perceptions include education, values, experience, and the school and community environment. Given the complexity and range of subscales and these internal and external factors, portfolios should focus on the criteria of perceived importance and skill level. These two self-assessments should be completed before beginning the digital portfolio process. This self-assessment is used differently depending on the user. For example, school leaders find their reflection on these scales useful in creating professional development activities. School leader candidates find their reflection on these scales useful in developing the internship experience. Because of the complexity of the ISLLC standards, this self-assessment provides focus for the digital portfolio and a rich source of information that is useful for planning and reflection. In chapter 6, you are asked to use the third scale to identify skill level at the end of the digital portfolio project.

Similarly, the TSSA technology self-assessment should be completed at the beginning and at the end of the digital portfolio process (see appendix B). As with the ISLLC self-assessment, the TSSA self-assessment is used differently by school leaders, school leader candidates, and school leadership faculty members. Using the first two scales, you identify the perceived importance of each element and perceived entry skill of each TSSA standard. Again, in chapter 6, you use the third scale to identify culminating skill levels at the end of the digital portfolio project.

ACTIVITY 2

Complete the perceived importance and the entry skill level scales of the ISLLC self-assessment (appendix A) and the TSSA self-assessment (appendix B). Compare and contrast the responses to each of these two instruments. Give particular attention to those elements that are considered very important but also have the lowest entry skill level. Those items should be considered priority subscales. Note these priority subscales as the ISLLC and TSSA standards worksheets are completed later in this chapter.

Review the examples of project-based activities for each standard. Identify objectives, activities, and artifacts for each standard.

After completing the ISSLC and the TSSA self-assessments, identify high-priority elements of the various standards. High priority is a function of perceived importance and entry skill level. School leaders might consider desired competence as a key factor in determining relative importance of the standards. Standards that are perceived as high in importance and low in skill level should be considered high-priority areas to address when developing the digital portfolio. Likewise, standards that are perceived as low in importance but high in skill level should be considered low-priority areas to address when developing the digital portfolio. There is not an exact formula to determine the elements of the standards that you should address, but self-assessment and careful reflection, based on the two criteria mentioned previously, provides focus for developing the portfolio. Fortunately there are several excellent resources for establishing priorities from these standards. For example, Capasso and Daresh (2001) provide excellent exercises and activities to facilitate developing specific projects and activities associated with the ISLLC standards. Martin, Wright, and Danzig (2003) offer exercises and activities to help address the ISLLC, TSSA, NCATE, and other standards and to help plan the school leader internship experience. Hackmann, Schmitt-Oliver, and Tracy (2002) provide an in-depth analysis of the ISLLC standards and an excellent array of activities and projects for each standard.

The ISLLC planner (see appendix C) and the TSSA planner (see appendix D) are tools that school leaders and school leader candidates can use to prioritize elements of these standards. For the next section, review the example objective, activities, and artifacts for each standard. The examples are only illustrative of the types of objectives, activities, and artifacts that you could consider and are far more comprehensive than most school leaders or school leader candidates would wish to complete. Therefore, consider the following examples as illustrative of the types of objectives, activities, and artifacts that can be included in a digital portfolio.

Also, consider the interrelationship among elements within each set of standards as well as the relationship between standards. For example, many of the objectives, activities, and artifacts for one element of a standard also relate to another element of that same standard. To illustrate, both the dispositions and performances for professional development are included in the sample worksheet for ISLLC standard 2. The personal professional development plan, the journal reflections, and the memorandums to the staff on professional development activities throughout the year are certainly related to dispositions. Many other activities and artifacts involved with this project, such as the memorandum to a school improvement planning committee, the professional development planning process and plans of the staff, and the budget and planning documents are all evidence of performances associated with this standard. In consideration of the ISLLC standards and the TSSA standards, school leaders and school leader candidates will likely make connections and hopefully derive new understandings of the interrelationship among professional standards. For instance, activities for ISLLC standard 1 include the use of technology as one way to communicate the vision and mission to the larger school community. Some of these same activities could be appropriate to the TSSA standard 1 as well. In the sample portfolios, the journal artifact for ISLLC standard 1 is also included as an artifact for TSSA standard 1. In sum, reflecting and understanding the connections among the standards is valuable for personal and professional growth during the digital portfolio process.

HOW IMPORTANT IS JOURNALING AND REFLECTION?

One of the most important elements of the digital portfolio process is journaling, reflection, and feedback. This aspect is important because consistently reflecting, journaling, and obtaining feedback from a critical friend provide examples for future use.

Dewey (1933) recognized the importance of reflection as the "active, persistent, and careful consideration of any belief or supposed form of knowledge in the light of the grounds that support it and the further conclusions to which it tends constitutes reflective thought" (p. 9). Valli (1997) identified five different types of reflection that could be used by school leaders and school leader candidates: "technical reflection, reflection-in and on-action, deliberative reflection, personalistic reflection, and critical reflection" (p. 5).

Technical reflection relates to the content of the reflection and the quality of the reflection. In this context, the ISLLC standards and the TSSA standards are used for reflection. A school leader or school leader candidate might reflect on a specific leadership task in a standard.

Reflection-in and on-action was first described by Schon (1983) in relation to teachers; however, this concept can be applied to school leaders and school leader candidates as well. Reflection-in-action is the careful consideration that occurs during the act of leadership. In contrast to technical reflection, from external standards, research, and best practices, reflection-in-action comes from the school leader's values and beliefs as well as the culture and context of the school and community. Reflection-on-action is the careful consideration that occurs after a leadership task has been completed. In this regard the reflection is derived from school leadership training and experience. Technical reflection is concerned with objective external norms, but reflection-in and on-action are more concerned with the unique dimensions associated with leadership in a particular school and community. Both reflection-in- and reflection-on-action emphasize the craft knowledge associated with school leadership.

According to Valli (1997), deliberative reflection comes from a variety of voices and perspectives including standards, research, experience, other school leaders, and values and beliefs. These different ways of describing school leader practice often lead to conflicting decisional alternatives for school leaders. It is the careful consideration of these options and their underlying sources of information that is the heart of deliberative reflection.

Personalistic reflection is heavily influenced by writing on the ethic of care (Noddings, 1984; Katz, Noddings, & Strike, 1999). It is also derived from the personal values, beliefs, and background of the school leader. In personalistic reflection, empathy toward members of the school community and compassion, trust, and loyalty is emphasized. In technical reflection, school leaders are concerned with professional standards and their universal application; however, in personalistic reflection, school leaders are concerned about the needs of the individual.

Critical reflection is drawn from the writings of critical theorists, such as Paulo Freire (1973), Henry Giroux (2001), and others, and is based on the premise that schooling contributes to social injustice and inequality. Through critical reflection, school leaders consider leadership behavior in the context of social activism to address the needs of the disempowered.

These five types of reflections might or might not be appropriate depending on the leadership activity. There could be instances in which all five types of reflection are useful for thinking about the leadership activity, and there could be other instances in which only one or two are appropriate. Carefully reflect on these five types of reflection when planning, implementing, assembling, and assessing the standards-based digital portfolio. The journal artifacts attached to the school leader sample portfolio provide examples of each different type of reflection.

HOW DO YOU USE THE ISLLC AND TSSA EXAMPLES AND WORKSHEETS?

Save the ISLLC Examples and Worksheets file and the TSSA Examples and Worksheets file from the accompanying CD to a diskette or hard drive. Also, access the ISLLC Examples Worksheets file and the TSSA Examples and Worksheets file in the Key Artifacts section of the Outline of the School Leader Template (explained in detail in chapter 5). Save each of these files under new names, for example, My ISLLC Worksheets and My TSSA Worksheets.

Once saved, complete the worksheets (figure 2.3 shows two copies of each: a completed sample and a blank) and hyperlink to a PowerPoint presentation or to TaskStream. The worksheets are provided as a visual illustration of how they can be used to take notes. In either digital or printed format, the worksheets are tools that school leaders and school leader candidates can use to strategize how to address selected elements of the standards in the digital portfolio.

Chapter 2

ISLLC Standard 1 Example					
A school administrator is an educational leader who promotes the success of all students by **facilitating the development, articulation, implementation, and stewardship of a vision of learning that is shared and supported by the school community.**				
Element	Priority	Objective	Activity	Artifact
Performances: The vision and mission of the school are effectively communicated to staff, parents, students, and community members	H	To establish a process for the dissemination of the shared school vision and mission to the school community	To collect and review the school vision and mission documents	Annotated compilation of school vision and mission documents Faculty meeting agenda PTO/PTA meeting agenda
			Update school website to include vision and mission and related documentation	Video Clip of vision and mission statement by school leader on school website
			Reflection on the implications of the vision and mission on leadership strategies and articulate to school community	Journal entries and feedback from critical friend

Figure 2.3. The ISLLC and TSSA Standard examples and worksheets (the sample portfolio can be accessed in the Resources folder of the accompanying CD)

ISLLC Standard 1 Worksheet				
A school administrator is an educational leader who promotes the success of all students by **facilitating the development, articulation, implementation, and stewardship of a vision of learning that is shared and supported by the school community.**				
Element	Priority	Objective	Activity	Artifact

Figure 2.3.   Continued

ISLLC Standard 2 Example

A school administrator is an educational leader who promotes the success of all students by **advocating, nurturing, and sustaining a school culture and instructional program conducive to student learning and staff professional growth.**

Element	Priority	Objective	Activity	Artifact
Dispositions: Professional development as an integral part of school improvements Performances: Professional development promotes a focus on student learning consistent with the school vision and goals	H	To demonstrate the importance of professional development through leading by example	Provide both oral and written communication to the school improvement planning committee charging them to carefully consider professional development in the planning process	Memorandum to the school improvement planning committee Meeting agendas School goal progress report
			Develop a personal professional development plan and share aspects of the plan with staff	Staff agenda Personal professional development plan Journal and feedback from critical friend
			Ensure that the professional development planning activities receive a high priority in the planning and budgetary processes	School improvement plan Budget documents
			Ensure professional plans for professional staff are aligned with school vision and goals	Staff professional plans
			Send personal notes to staff throughout the year related to participation in professional development activities	Memorandums

Figure 2.3. Continued

ISLLC Standard 2 Worksheet			
A school administrator is an educational leader who promotes the success of all students by **advocating, nurturing, and sustaining a school culture and instructional program conducive to student learning and staff professional growth.**			
Element	Priority	Objective	Activity	Artifact

Figure 2.3. Continued

ISLLC Standard 3 Example					
A school administrator is an educational leader who promotes the success of all students by **ensuring management of the organization, operations, and resources for a safe, efficient, and effective learning environment.**					
Element	Priority	Objective	Activity	Artifact	
Knowledge: Principles and issues relating to school safety and security	H	To audit the school safety and security policies and procedures and implement changes in light of best practice at the district, state, and national levels	Form a school safety and security committee as a standing committee	Charge to committee members	
			Give the committee the responsibility to review school, district, state, and national safety and security policies and procedures	Compilation of policies including faculty handbook, student handbook, and school and district safety plans.	
				Compilation of guidelines from appropriate state and national agencies	
			Charge the committee to make recommendations based on best practices	Committee agenda	
			Assist the committee in conducting focus group meetings with members of the school community to identify concerns	Focus group agendas and reports	
			Review recommendations from committee with the faculty	Committee report	
				Agenda of meeting with faculty	
			Reflection	Journal entries and feedback from critical friend	

Figure 2.3. Continued

ISLLC Standard 3 Worksheet				
A school administrator is an educational leader who promotes the success of all students by **ensuring management of the organization, operations, and resources for a safe, efficient, and effective learning environment.**				
Element	Priority	Objective	Activity	Artifact

Figure 2.3. Continued

ISLLC Standard 4 Example

A school administrator is an educational leader who promotes the success of all students by **collaborating with families and community members, responding to diverse community interests and needs, and mobilizing community resources.**

Element	Priority	Objective	Activity	Artifact
Performances: A comprehensive program of community relations is established	H	To develop, implement, and evaluate a school community relations program	Review relevant school, district, and state policy	Compilation of relevant school, district, and state policies
			Review policies and procedures recommended by the National School Public Relations Association and other professional associations	Annotated bibliography of "best practices" associated with school community relations policy and procedures
			Establish a school community relations committee and assign a relations coordinator	Memorandum describing membership and duties of school community relations committee
				Job description of the school community relations coordinator
			Recommend modifications to current policy	Memorandum to central office with list of recommended changes to current school and district policy
			Establish and implement a school community plan	School community relations plan
				Agendas and minutes
				Newsletter
				School improvement plan
			Reflection	Journal entries and feedback from critical friend

Figure 2.3. Continued

ISLLC Standard 4 Worksheet			
A school administrator is an educational leader who promotes the success of all students by **collaborating with families and community members, responding to diverse community interests and needs, and mobilizing community resources.**			
Element	Priority	Objective	Activity	Artifact

Figure 2.3. Continued

ISLLC Standard 5 Example			
A school administrator is an educational leader who promotes the success of all students by **acting with integrity, fairness, and in an ethical manner.**			
Element	Priority	Objective	Activity	Artifact
Dispositions: bringing ethical principles to the decision-making process	H	Develop, implement, and evaluate ethical decision-making processes	Conduct a review of the literature on the ethic of justice, the ethic of critique, the ethic of care, and the ethic profession	Annotated bibliography of resources on the four ethical paradigms
			Read and reflect on representative material for each of the four ethics	Journal entries and feedback from critical friend
			Identify a critical friend to share readings, reflections, and feedback	Document meeting times and dates

Summary of feedback and statements articulating new meaning and understandings |
| | | | Present a professional development workshop on the application of the four ethical paradigms in decision making | Handouts

PowerPoint presentation

Evaluations from attendees |

Figure 2.3. Continued

ISLLC Standard 5 Worksheet				
A school administrator is an educational leader who promotes the success of all students by **acting with integrity, fairness, and in an ethical manner.**				
Element	Priority	Objective	Activity	Artifact

Figure 2.3. Continued

ISLLC Standard 6 Example				
A school administrator is an educational leader who promotes the success of all students by **understanding, responding to, and influencing the larger political, social, economic, legal, and cultural context.**				
Element	Priority	Objective	Activity	Artifact
Knowledge: The importance of diversity and equity in a democratic society	H	To develop and implement a personal professional plan for investigating the role and function of diversity and equity in American society	Conduct a literature review to identify a list of contemporary readings on the role and function of equity and diversity in education in America	Bibliography of resources
			Select a series of readings to complete over the course of the school year	Annotations associated with each reading
			Investigate data associated with the impact of racial ethic, gender, SES, and other factors on educational access and student achievement at the local, state, and national level	Summary of U.S. Department of Education, U.S. Census, state, and local data and implications for selected school populations
			Read and reflect on each reading and consider the implications for leadership	Journal entries and feedback from critical friend

Figure 2.3. Continued

ISLLC Standard 6 Worksheet				
A school administrator is an educational leader who promotes the success of all students by **understanding, responding to, and influencing the larger political, social, economic, legal, and cultural context.**				
Element	Priority	Objective	Activity	Artifact

Figure 2.3. Continued

The TSSA Standard 1 Example

Leadership and Vision: Educational leaders inspire a shared vision for comprehensive integration of technology and foster an environment and culture conducive to the realization of that vision.

Educational leaders	Priority	Objective	Activity	Artifacts
Facilitate the shared development by all stakeholders of a vision for technology use and widely communicate that vision	H	Create a school technology vision statement consistent with district, state, and national policy and best practice	Solicit recommendations from school and community constituencies	Letter to constituent groups inviting nominations
			Establish an ad hoc school community technology committee	List of nominees
			Provide committee charge related to review of district, state, and national policies to identify best practices and to prepare draft vision statement	Memorandum to committee with appointment and charge
			Solicit feedback from various school community stakeholders	Agenda and minutes from constituent groups
				Comments received from school website
				Notes from focus groups
			Submit technology vision and mission statement to central office for approval	Draft technology vision mission statement
				Memorandum to central office
			Submit technology vision and mission statement to school board for approval	Board agenda
			Reflection	Journal entries and feedback from critical friend

Figure 2.3. Continued

TSSA Standard 1 Worksheet				
Leadership and Vision: Educational leaders inspire a shared vision for comprehensive integration of technology and foster an environment and culture conducive to the realization of that vision.				
Educational leaders	Priority	Objective	Activity	Artifact

Figure 2.3. Continued

TSSA Standard 2 Example				
Learning and Teaching: Educational leaders ensure that curricular design, instructional strategies, and learning environments integrate appropriate technologies to maximize learning and teaching.				
Educational leaders	Priority	Objective	Activity	Artifact
Provide for learner-centered environments that use technology to meet the individual and diverse needs of learners	H	Develop a technology facilities audit and plan	Screen and select a technology consultant to develop technology facilities plan	Request for proposal
			Technology consultant conducts equipment and facilities audit	Technology facilities audit report
			Technology consultant conducts survey of school staff	Survey results
			Technology consultant develops draft plan	Draft plan
			Technology facilities plan is reviewed by school staff	Agendas and meeting minutes
			Technology facilities plan is submitted to central office for approval	Technology facilities plan

Memorandum to central office |
| | | | Technology facilities plan submitted to school board for approval | Board agenda

Minutes

PowerPoint presentation |
| | | | Reflection | Journal entries and feedback from critical friend |

Figure 2.3. Continued

TSSA Standard 2 Worksheet				
Learning and Teaching: Educational leaders ensure that curricular design, instructional strategies, and learning environments integrate appropriate technologies to maximize learning and teaching.				
Educational leaders	Priority	Objective	Activity	Artifact

Figure 2.3. Continued

TSSA Standard 3 Example				
Productivity and Professional Practice: Educational leaders apply technology to enhance their professional practice and to increase their own productivity and that of others.				
Educational leaders	Priority	Objective	Activity	Artifact
Employ technology for communication and collaboration among colleagues, staff members, parents, students, and the larger community		To use technology to communicate to the school community on selected topics	Update school website to include vision and mission and related documentation	Video clip of vision and mission statement by school leader on school website E-mail link to facilitate communication regarding vision and mission.
			Curriculum objectives and activities made available online	School website
			Reflection	Journal entries and feedback from critical friend

Figure 2.3. Continued

TSSA Standard 3 Worksheet				
Productivity and Professional Practice: Educational leaders apply technology to enhance their professional practice and to increase their own productivity and that of others.				
Educational leaders	Priority	Objective	Activity	Artifact

Figure 2.3. Continued

TSSA Standard 4 Example			
Support, Management, and Operations: Educational leaders ensure the integration of technology to support productive systems for learning and administration.			
Educational leaders	Priority	Objective	Activity	Artifact
Implement procedures to drive continuous improvement of technology systems and to support technology replacement cycles	H	Develop a technology replacement cycle	Charge technology coordinator to draft proposed technology replacement policy and procedures	Memorandum
			Technology coordinator conducts review of relevant school, district, and state policies and procedures	School, district, and state policies and procedures
			Technology professional development meeting with instructional staff	Agenda PowerPoint presentation Handouts Minutes
			Review and revise draft technology replacement policy and procedures submitted by technology coordinator	Draft policy and procedures
			Policy and procedures reviewed by central office	Recommended policy and procedures Memorandum
			Policy and procedures submitted to school board	Board agenda Minutes
			Reflection	Journal entries and feedback from critical friend

Figure 2.3. Continued

TSSA Standard 4 Worksheet				
Support, Management, and Operations: Educational leaders ensure the integration of technology to support productive systems for learning and administration.				
Educational leaders	Priority	Objective	Activity	Artifact

Figure 2.3.   Continued

TSSA Standard 5 Example

Assessment and Evaluation: Educational leaders use technology to plan and implement comprehensive systems of effective assessment and evaluation.

Educational leaders	Priority	Objective	Activity	Artifact
Assess staff knowledge, skills, and performance in using technology and use results to facilitate quality professional development and to inform personnel decisions	H	Develop and implement a plan to assess staff knowledge, skills, and performances using technology	Review relevant school and district contract and personnel policies	School and district personnel and technology policies Collective bargaining agreements
			With the assistance of the technology coordinator develop a technology proficiency assessment completed by all new and continuing instructional staff	Proficiency assessment
			Review aggregated multiyear results to identify staff technology development needs and share with staff development committee	Summary of results Agenda Minutes
			Include technology proficiency as a factor in hiring new staff	Individual proficiency results
			Reflection	Journal entries and feedback from critical friend

Figure 2.3. Continued

TSSA Standard 5 Worksheet				
Assessment and Evaluation: Educational leaders use technology to plan and implement comprehensive systems of effective assessment and evaluation.				
Educational leaders	Priority	Objective	Activity	Artifact

Figure 2.3. Continued

TSSA Standard 6 Example			
Social, Legal, and Ethical Issues: Educational leaders understand the social, legal, and ethical issues related to technology and model responsible decision making related to these issues.			
Educational leaders	Priority	Objective	Activity	Artifact
Promote and enforce environmentally safe and healthy practices in the use of technology	H	Develop and implement policies and procedures that reflect an environmentally responsible use of technology	Review relevant school, district, state, and EPA guidelines	School, district, state, and EPA policies
			Hire a consultant	Request for proposal
			Technology consultant recommendations related to the following technology issues: hazardous waste, recycling, energy efficiency, and cost efficiency	Consultant report and recommendations
			Technology committee develops draft policy and procedures	Agenda Minutes Draft policy and procedures
			Review proposed policy and procedures with staff	Instructional and classified staff meeting agenda Minutes
			Incorporate policy and procedures into the orientation and mentoring of new staff members	Handout PowerPoint presentation Mentoring training video clip
			Reflection	Journal entries and feedback from critical friend

Figure 2.3.   Continued

TSSA Standard 6 Worksheet				
Social, Legal, and Ethical Issues: Educational leaders understand the social, legal, and ethical issues related to technology and model responsible decision making related to these issues.				
Educational leaders	Priority	Objective	Activity	Artifact

Figure 2.3. Continued

Now begin to assemble the standards-based digital portfolio. You have already completed the following steps in this process:

1. The development of an individualized definition of the standards-based digital portfolio.
2. The review, reflection, and possible modification of the outline template.

3. The completion of the standards self-assessments and the identification of priorities.
4. The review of example projects for each standard.
5. The development of proposed objectives, activities, and artifacts for each standard.
6. The development of a digital filing system for the portfolio. This step warrants thorough consideration. Although there is no right or wrong method of filing, file names should be brief and clear to assist you with assembling and others with viewing the digital portfolio. Consider creating a folder for each standard in My Documents on your computer hard drive. Within each folder include all files associated with that standard. Remember that some artifacts can meet more than one standard and, therefore, need to be hyperlinked to other standards as well. File naming is critical in setting up a useful filing system. For more details, see p. 54.
7. Linking the digital assembly of objectives, activities, and artifacts to each standard. There are many different ways to do this, but a simple and effective way is to copy the objectives and activities from the worksheets to the appropriate slides. The artifacts will be hyperlinked to the various standards slides.
8. The continuous reflection and modification of the design, which effects changes based on personal preferences, technical proficiency, and reflection and feedback from a critical friend. With regard to this last point, the formative evaluation rubric can be used to evaluate your work or it can be shared with a critical friend to receive feedback (see appendix E). The formative evaluation rubric guides reflective assessment while the portfolio is being developed. School leaders and school leader candidates benefit from using this instrument at various stages in the development of the digital portfolio.

SUMMARY

In this chapter we provided an introduction to the digital portfolio outline template and an overview of a linear and nonlinear outline format. We explored how to alter the outline template consistent with personalized definitions. Upon completing the ISLLC and TSSA standards self-assessments, priority elements were identified. Subsequent to a review of example projects for each standard, project-based activities were formulated, including objectives, activities, and artifacts. You are now prepared to assemble the standards-based digital portfolio.

Review the completed planning worksheets with a critical friend and consider the following questions:

- Are the plans feasible in terms of your time and resources (and the time and resources of others involved)?
- Do the objectives, activities, and artifacts address the identified priorities?
- How will artifacts be labeled, filed, and stored?
- What are the issues and concerns? Explore these with a critical friend.

Complete the formative evaluation rubric (appendix E) at various stages in the development process. Also, have a critical friend complete the rubric each time. Compare and contrast your responses with the responses of the critical friend. Identify strengths as well as opportunities for improvement. Develop strategies to address opportunities for improvement.

Chapter Three

Digital Format Options

This chapter provides an overview of the technology involved to prepare a digital portfolio. In particular, we discuss computer requirements for producing digital portfolios, peripheral hardware that might be needed, development software, and storage mediums for saving and distributing portfolios. By the end of this chapter, you will be prepared to select a digital format for your portfolio.

Just as physical portfolios usually include sections, tabs, and artifacts, digital portfolios include virtual equivalents of these elements. One of the advantages of digital portfolios is that they allow viewers to choose the order in which sections are viewed, like an Internet site. This interaction has the potential to draw in audiences more readily than with physical portfolios. Another appealing aspect is that digital portfolios can include anything that can be stored on a computer—documents, pictures, audio clips, videos, or combinations of these. Although most artifacts in digital portfolios are text, a digital format can contain anything that can be digitized—including publications, snapshots, and videos. Portfolios are presented through software. Once complete, they are stored on digital mediums (Internet, CD, or diskette) that allow easy access for all potential audiences.

WHAT KIND OF COMPUTER DO I NEED?

To develop a digital portfolio, you can use either a Macintosh or a computer running Windows. The more recent the computer and operating system, the easier the project will be. This book is written with a Macintosh running OS X or a PC running Windows 2000 or Windows XP in mind. Most of the examples—and all of the instructions in chapters 4 and 5—are drawn from a PC and from Office 2000 or above. If using a Macintosh or other software, adjust these instructions accordingly.

Specifically, we recommend the following PC configuration: Windows 2000 or Windows XP; 512 MB RAM minimum (1 GB RAM will speed and facilitate the process); and 40 MB hard drive, particularly if the portfolio process involves video editing (see below).

WHAT HARDWARE DO I NEED TO PRODUCE A SCHOOL LEADER PORTFOLIO?

The type of artifacts in the portfolio determines what hardware is required. The following is a list of peripherals useful in preparing different types of artifacts.

Scanners

Artifacts that are not already in digital format can be converted by using a scanner. Scanners convert photos, drawings, papers, and news articles—anything that can be photocopied. Scanned pictures can be cropped so that they include only the most significant part of the image. The process for scanning pictures and photos is different from scanning documents; so, be sure to read the scanner directions before beginning. Documents can be scanned and converted into word processor text or they can be scanned as pictures. However, when documents are scanned as pictures, they often lose quality. Try a few sample scans before including pictures of documents.

Cameras

Digital still cameras vary considerably, but all offer different resolutions for the pictures they take. The highest resolution is suitable for quality photographic prints, and the lowest is suitable for e-mail inserts. For a digital portfolio, choose something in the middle (see the discussion of digital pictures below). Remember, the higher the resolution, the larger the photo and file size. Consider carefully before adding artifacts that are very large in size because they restrict the number of artifacts that can be added. In other words, save file space where possible. You might want to (or need to, depending on the camera) process digital photos using a photo-imaging program. Save photos as *.jpg files; this format works best with Web pages and presentation software. Cameras vary in their options for saving pictures. Some cameras allow saving in e-mail format, which provides smaller, lower quality images that work well in a digital portfolio. Read the manual and take sample pictures in various resolutions.

Video Cameras

Video artifacts rivet portfolio reviewers, particularly if they cover critical events or illustrate a point well. If using a digital camcorder, download the video directly into the computer using a cable supplied with the camera. If both camera and computer support FireWire (on the Mac) or IEEE 1394—a very fast external bus that is ideal for transferring videos—the transfer is simple and relatively quick. If not using a digital camera, hardware and software that converts the analog videos to digital format is required. Many still cameras are capable of making two to three minute videos. When using this option, check the manual to ensure that the camera's memory is sufficient for videos.

CD Recorder

To save work to a CD, you need a CD recorder—sometimes called a CD burner—in the computer. CD-R (compact disc-recordable) drives burn data to a CD until it is full, but it cannot be rewritten or reused. CD-RW (compact disc-rewriteable) drives rewrite data to a CD, just like floppy disks. Both CD formats hold 650–700 MB, but the physical structure of the discs is very different and not interchangeable. As you work, save to a CD-RW; however, if working on more than one computer, know that sometimes there are compatibility problems with CD-RW drives on different computers. When the portfolio is complete and it is time to make copies for distribution, we recommend using a CD-R. This disc can be recorded on either a CD-R drive or a CD-RW drive.

Flash Drive

If using more than one computer to produce a portfolio—or if you desire a portable portfolio—purchase a flash drive. These thumb-sized, portable hard drives are recognized by any computer operating system that has the plug-and-play feature (Windows 2000, Windows XP, Mac OS X). The drive plugs into a USB port, is recognized by the computer, and functions as a removable hard drive. Flash drives have capacities of 32 MB up to 1 GB, are readily available, and have become very reasonable. If the flash drive will be used to store videos, we suggest a size of at least 256 MB.

Audio Recorder

Using audio files in the portfolio necessitates either a digital audio recorder or an audio card and software that allow moving audio from tapes to digital files.

HOW DO I SAVE THE PORTFOLIO AS IT'S DEVELOPED?

While working on portfolios, you make connections, or links, between its various elements. To ensure that the finished product works well, create a filing system from the very beginning. A properly created filing system permits you to transfer the portfolio from one drive to another and from one computer to another and still know that the links all work. Creating links on a computer involves setting the path to a file (drive\folder\file, e.g., C:\portfoliodk\video1). If a file is later moved from one folder to another, all links to that file will need to be reset. To avoid this potentially arduous task, take time initially to plan the filing system.

Whether using a computer hard drive, a flash drive, a floppy disk, or a CD, the first task is to create a folder to hold everything.

1. If the folder is on a flash drive, double click the My Computer icon on the desktop, and then double click the icon for the removable drive. If the folder will be on the desktop, simply leave the cursor on the desktop.

2. Right click on the open space of either the flash drive list or the desktop.
3. Scroll down to New and left click.
4. From the options that appear, choose New Folder.
5. When the folder appears, the title New Folder is highlighted. Type the new name and press the Enter key.

Keep the folder name simple—your last name, "portfolio," and initials (no spaces) or something similarly distinctive. Every part of the portfolio should be in this folder. Create this folder once.

Next, create folders within this master folder. These secondary folders can be titled for standards (standard1, standard2, etc.) or for artifacts (e.g., essays, plans, photos, or videos). If material is organized into standards folders, store videos, pictures, or graphics in one central folder, this enables you to use a graphic in various parts of the portfolio while storing only one copy of it. Remember, only one copy of an artifact is necessary in the portfolio; you can link to that artifact from any place in the portfolio as long as you can locate it. Add folders as needed, and delete unused folders at any time.

Finally, fill the folders with artifacts and elements for the portfolio. Keep file names simple and brief. When naming files, be sure that they are intuitively obvious; opening a document to determine what it contains breaks the creative flow of portfolio design. Because it is likely that school leaders will have more than one objective for each standard, code the objectives, activities, and artifacts by numbers or letters so that they associate with each other and are clearly identified. See chapters 4 and 5 for specific recommendations for labeling files.

HOW DO I USE DIGITAL PICTURES IN A PORTFOLIO?

First, when taking digital pictures, decide on the quality desired. Digital cameras allow a choice of resolution, and resolution determines quality. Resolution also affects the file size—the higher the resolution, the larger the file. Some cameras allow you to choose the pixel size of an image (a megapixel equals more than a million pixels). For digital use, the smaller size, usually 640 × 480, is sufficient. If digital pictures are to be printed, use higher resolutions (up to 1216 × 912). If the camera offers resolution in terms of dots per inch (dpi), choose lower resolutions; computer screens usually display 72–100 dpi, and printers print 300 (dots per inch) / dpi or more. Also, this lower resolution produces an image that loads quickly and fits on the computer screen; pictures with higher resolutions often extend beyond the sides of the screen and cannot be viewed without scrolling. To include high-resolution pictures in the portfolio, bring the image into a photo-editing program and save it in a lower resolution.

Getting the images from a digital camera into a computer is easy. Although digital cameras store images on a variety of media (memory stick, SmartMedia card, MultiMedia card, and even floppy disk and CD), most digital cameras have USB or serial connections that allow direct transfer to the computer; and, if the camera uses a floppy disk or CD, insert directly into the computer and read from it. In some cases, the download can be initiated from the camera; in others, a photo editor is necessary to begin the download. Check the manual for the camera first.

Finally, remember that photo artifacts are more effective if they show action and if they show people doing something related to a standard; otherwise, the result is a scrapbook rather than a portfolio. Use a photo-editing program to crop the picture, adjust the brightness and contrast, and otherwise tinker with the image so that it effectively communicates what is desired.

HOW CAN I DIGITIZE AND USE 35 MM PHOTOGRAPHS?

If there are only a few images, this is a job for a scanner. Check the scanner manual for operations because scanners are either started by a button or launched from software. Some computers and scanners are configured to permit a choice of programs to scan a file; if the choice includes photo-editing software, use it and save a step. The software might ask what type of image is being scanned—color photo, grayscale, or line art. Black-and-white photos and newspaper photos are grayscale, and handwriting or black-and-white artwork is line art. Launching the software that accompanies the scanner will prescan the image. From the prescan, select the area that is desired in a similar process to cropping a digital photo. Before clicking the Scan button, check the resolution setting (as with digital photos, the higher the resolution, the larger the photo and the larger the file) and the format. Formats for photos vary considerably. They include the following:

jpeg: a compressed format with lots of color variation, which is particularly good for the Internet and for on-screen viewing
gif: good for on-screen viewing and best suited to line art and flat colors—much less color variation than jpeg
tiff: a universal format that works on PCs and Macs—file sizes are usually quite large, and the format does not work on the Web.
pict: a Mac-only uncompressed format

Once the photo is scanned into the computer, it can be manipulated just as if it were a photo taken with a digital camera. If planning to take more pictures with 35 mm film, there are a number of options for digitizing them. Most developers—from Kodak to the local drugstore—offer the option of obtaining photos on a picture CD in a number of different formats. Often, the CD also has software for editing the pictures. Try one of these CD services before committing to it for portfolio photos.

HOW CAN I DIGITIZE AND USE VIDEOS ON A VHS TAPE?

Converting analog videos into digital videos requires a video digitizer (hardware) and a video-editing program (software). The digitizer can be built into the computer or it can be an external device. In either case, connect "video out" from the VCR or camcorder to the "video in" of the digitizer, using ordinary RCA cables. Adding a digitizer to a computer requires installing a digital video card into the CPU. A number of digitizers are available for Windows systems, the most popular of which are made by Dazzle and Pinnacle Systems. Both of those cards come with video-editing software. Most Macintosh computers have digital video capability built into them, and both Mac and Windows XP include video-editing capabilities (iMovie on the Mac and Movie Maker on Windows XP).

Editing involves bringing the video onto a storyboard, choosing the frames to be used, adding captions or voice-over, and saving. One significant difference between professional videos and home videos is editing: professional videos are cut so that only the critical parts of the action are included, while home videos include *everything*. Limit video clips so they will load quickly and communicate effectively (so the viewer isn't tempted to end them prematurely). Clips should effectively communicate about a standard in thirty to ninety seconds.

Both Apple and Microsoft provide tutorials and helpful hints on their websites. For Microsoft, go to www.microsoft.com/windowsxp/using/moviemaker/default.mspx; for Mac, go to http://ali.apple.com/ali_sites/ali/exhibits/1000019.

IS THE PROCESS OF USING A DIGITAL VIDEO CAMERA ANY DIFFERENT?

The process of downloading the video from the camera into the computer is different. Because the video is in digital format, it is ready to be moved to the computer, and most digital video recorders (including still cameras that take short videos) come with a FireWire or IEEE 1394 connection, which provides fast downloads. Check the connectors because FireWire connectors can have four or six pins. The correct cable makes it easy to connect the camera to the computer, run the software, and download the video. Be sure to edit the video for a more professional look and length.

WHICH SOFTWARE SHOULD I USE TO PRESENT THE PORTFOLIO?

If a school leader designs the portfolio, there are three main software choices: presentation software, Web editors, and an online service. If the portfolio is designed as part of a class or a program, the class instructor might choose software. The choice is determined by the computer literacy of the portfolio designer. We address three software approaches to portfolios: presentation software, an online service, and a Web page editor.

Presentation software is most familiar, both for audiences and designers. Many computers come with PowerPoint (the most common presentation software program), and learning to use the program is fairly easy. Presentation software unifies the graphic theme for the portfolio and is viewed on a computer screen. A PowerPoint portfolio, in addition to including slides that highlight achievements or abilities, can perform other tasks, such as making links out of text or graphics on a slide; using links to launch other applications and display a document, picture, or video; linking slides with buttons (like websites); and creating navigation buttons (e.g., Back, Next). Chapter 4 fully explores these various options.

When finished, the portfolio presentation can be saved with a viewer, and the audience does not need the program in order to view it. However, the audience will need the word processing program that produced the documents to view the presentation. It is possible to e-mail a portfolio created in presentation software; however, the portfolio folder must be compressed by the portfolio designer and then uncompressed by the recipient. Save a portfolio done in presentation software in a medium that can be handed to the recipient.

A second possible type of software is a Web editor. With a Web editor, you can create Web pages without knowledge of HTML (hypertext markup language), the computer language in which they are created. A Web page portfolio can be run on any computer that has a Web browser on it, which is virtually all computers. Web format is instantly recognizable to anyone who has used the Internet, and navigation of websites is second nature to most computer users. Most Web editors are "what you see is what you get," and unless you are willing to learn the complexities of HTML, these are recommended. Simple Web editors such as Netscape Composer and Microsoft FrontPage Express are available for free download, and many computers have them as part of their software packages. Full-featured Web editors such as Macromedia Dreamweaver, Microsoft FrontPage, and Adobe PageMill offer more capabilities and more complexity; they can create Web pages with frames, they offer drag-and-drop functionality, and they include wizards that guide you through a good deal of the process. Linking documents, pictures, and videos is relatively simple, and a Web page portfolio can also include links to the Internet. Documents in the portfolio can be run in their original programs (if the viewer's computer includes those programs) or they can easily be converted into HTML and displayed as Web pages.

A third software possibility is the online service. This book includes a subscription to one online service, TaskStream. Instructions for accessing the complimentary TaskStream account are provided in chapter 5.

WHAT ARE THE ADVANTAGES AND DISADVANTAGES OF VARIOUS STORAGE MEDIA?

Floppy disks are the simplest storage medium. Everyone is familiar with them, and they fit many computers. They also hold the least information—1.2 MB. A good deal of text can be stored on a floppy disk, but graphics reduce the space quickly, and audio and video files are prohibitively large (about three minutes of video will fill the disk). Floppy disks might appear to be a universal storage medium, but current laptops and some newer desktops do not have floppy disk drives.

CDs hold much more information. Their 650 MB equals more than 500 floppy disks. All computers come with a CD drive, which makes portfolios accessible to anyone with a computer. In addition, it is possible to create a self-booting CD that launches itself when placed in the drive. A CD can store Web pages or presentations, either of which can be run from the CD. This is an excellent medium for publishing and distributing the final portfolio, but it is not efficient for day-to-day storage and work.

Finally, if the portfolio is a Web page, it can be stored on an Internet server and accessed via the Internet. If the portfolio is created using an online service such as TaskStream, it is stored on the server of the online service. A host is required to post a Web page portfolio on the Internet. Some schools and universities provide their employees and students with Web space to create Web pages free of charge. Free Web space is also available from a number of Internet hosts. To get the space, you have to agree that your page will include the host's advertisements (the host controls ad content). If you use a site with free hosting, first access a page hosted at the site to see that it loads quickly and includes appropriate ads. A final option is to pay for a host. A quick search of the Internet provides thousands of possibilities.

CONCLUSION

The software decision is the most important. Review the following requirements for PowerPoint and TaskStream based on needs, abilities, and willingness to try new approaches. PowerPoint requires

- familiarity with word processing and graphics,
- distribution of a CD by mail or other physical means,
- more storage space for the final product,
- preparing a list of linking standards,
- learning and using built-in hypermedia features, and
- viewers with programs in which to view artifacts.

TaskStream requires

- familiarity with using the Internet,
- distribution via the World Wide Web,
- no local storage space for the final product,
- linking to standards lists provided by TaskStream,
- hypermedia linking provided by TaskStream, and
- programs for viewing artifacts that are generally compatible with Web pages.

ACTIVITY: TECHNOLOGY SELF-ASSESSMENT

Preparing a digital portfolio requires various skills. The self-assessment in figure 3.1 provides an insight into those skills. Following each skill is a rating scale ranging from adept (5) to neophyte (1). After completing the activity, read the following interpretation.

Item Interpretation

A rating of four or below indicates a need for extra learning in an area. Although that learning can extend the time required to produce a digital portfolio, the result will be stronger, thanks to a more diverse set of artifacts, clearer organization, and smoother functionality.

		Adept		Competent		Neophyte
1.	Writing/editing in a word processor	5	4	3	2	1
2.	Moving/copying computer files	5	4	3	2	1
3.	Creating tables in a word processor	5	4	3	2	1
4.	Creating PowerPoint presentations	5	4	3	2	1
5.	Linking other files to a presentation	5	4	3	2	1
6.	Navigating the Internet	5	4	3	2	1
7.	Uploading files to the Internet	5	4	3	2	1
8.	Creating Web pages	5	4	3	2	1
9.	Inserting hotlinks in a document/page	5	4	3	2	1
10.	Shooting digital photos	5	4	3	2	1
11.	Editing digital photos	5	4	3	2	1
12.	Shooting digital videos	5	4	3	2	1
13.	Editing digital videos	5	4	3	2	1
14.	Recording sound digitally	5	4	3	2	1
15.	Inserting sound files in a document	5	4	3	2	1

Add and total the columns: ____ + ____ + ____ + ____ + ____ = ____

Overall rating is as follows: Adept: 75 to 56, Competent: 55 to 36, Neophyte: 35 to 15.

Figure 3.1. Technology self-assessment

Overall Rating

An overall rating of adept or competent suggests that you should strongly consider the TaskStream version of the digital portfolio. Since TaskStream provides more technology options, it is more suitable for the more technologically skilled. An overall rating of competent or neophyte suggests that you might be more comfortable using the PowerPoint version. Those selecting the PowerPoint version are familiar with the Microsoft Office suite of software but are not skilled in using the Internet or other software programs.

Chapter Four

The PowerPoint Option

Chapter 3 culminated in an activity in which you selected one of two preferred digital format options: PowerPoint or TaskStream. Chapter 4 is written specifically for those who select PowerPoint as the preferred standards-based digital portfolio tool. This chapter also reviews basic Microsoft Office PowerPoint 2003 functions and steps to begin assembling the standards-based digital portfolio.

REVIEW OF BASIC POWERPOINT FUNCTIONS

We do not provide basic technology training but we suggest how technology can be used when developing a standards-based digital portfolio. Therefore, this chapter does not provide PowerPoint training. If you have questions about using and modifying the outline template, refer to the PowerPoint Help files or Microsoft's online PowerPoint training at http://office.microsoft.com/assistance/. In addition, Montgomery and Wiley (2004) provide a thorough exploration of PowerPoint functions.

PowerPoint 2003 is a graphics presentation program included in the Microsoft Office suite of programs. Review the software and hardware configurations on your computer because variations can affect functionality. In particular, earlier software versions of PowerPoint might not run files produced on later versions, but later versions will typically run files produced on earlier versions. In order to open PowerPoint, turn the computer on, left click on the Start icon at the bottom left corner of the screen, place the cursor over the text All Programs, and right click on PowerPoint 2003.

You can also open PowerPoint by creating a shortcut on the screen. To create a shortcut to PowerPoint, click on the Start button at the bottom left of the screen, right click on All Programs, right click on Microsoft Office, right click on Microsoft Office PowerPoint 2003, and left click on Create Shortcut.

ACCESSING THE STANDARDS-BASED SCHOOL LEADER DIGITAL PORTFOLIO TEMPLATE

First, create a folder for the digital portfolio project files, including the School Leader Portfolio Template and all digital artifacts (see pp. 54–55). This folder is particularly important for making copies of the portfolio for review. Unless the artifacts and the PowerPoint presentation are in the same folder, reviewers can only access the PowerPoint presentation. To create a folder, right click in an open area of the desktop. Scroll down to the New icon, and left click on Folder. A New Folder icon will appear. Place the cursor in the text field under the icon and backspace to erase the text and rename.

The CD enclosed with this book includes both the School Leader Portfolio Template and the School Leader Sample Portfolio. Complete the following steps to access the standards-based digital portfolio template. Place the CD in the CD drive. Left click twice on My Computer, left click twice on the CD drive, and left click twice on the folder titled School Leader Portfolio Template. Once the PowerPoint file is open, save a copy of the file for your own use and adaptation as follows: select the File menu in the menu bar, scroll down and left click once on the Save As icon, select the folder in which the file is to be saved in the Save In field, rename in the file name field, and left click once on the Save icon.

ADDING OBJECTIVES, ACTIVITIES, AND ARTIFACTS TO THE DIGITAL PORTFOLIO

The central components of the portfolio are the objectives, activities, and artifacts documented for each standard. One way to construct the portfolio is provided below. Note that the example objectives, activities, and artifacts for the ISLLC and TSSA standards are included in the School Leader Sample Portfolio on the accompanying CD.

Prior to adding objectives, activities, and artifacts to the digital portfolio, complete the worksheets in chapter 2. The ISLLC Examples Worksheets file and the TSSA Examples and Worksheets file are located in the Supplemental Material/Resources page in the Outline of the School Leader Template. Open and save each of these files under a new file name, either on a disk or computer hard drive. For the following illustration, we assume the ISLLC Examples and Worksheets are saved on the hard drive as My ISLLC Worksheets, and the TSSA Examples and Worksheets are saved on the hard drive as My TSSA Worksheets. To add the text for objectives and activities, copy and paste to the School Leader Digital Portfolio as follows:

1. Complete and save the ISLLC and TSSA Worksheets (see chapter 2).
2. Open the file and select the completed worksheet. Place cursor in the desired column at the beginning of text that is to be added. Holding down the left mouse button, scroll and highlight the text.
3. Left click the Edit menu and left click on Copy.
4. Open the School Leader Digital Portfolio. Left click once on the View menu to make sure file is in Normal View.
5. In the Outline or Slide Screen in the left inset box, select the slide and the desired standard.
6. Place the cursor immediately after the word Objectives or Activities where the text is to be added. Left click once and a gray highlighted box will appear indicating that the selected area of the slide can be edited.
7. Place the cursor on the Edit icon, scroll down, and left click on the Paste icon. The typeface will appear much larger. Highlight the selected text and select size 16-point font or other desired font size in the formatting tool bar above the slide. See the School Leader Sample Portfolio for examples of the results of this process.

More than likely, you will have more than one objective for the standards and should code the objectives, activities, and artifacts by numbers and letters so that they are clearly identified. For example, the first objective under any given standard can be labeled "1," the second objective "2," and so on. If there are two activities associated with objective 1, they can be labeled "1.A" and "1.B." If there are two artifacts associated with activity 1.A, they can be labeled "1.A.1" and "1.A.2." If there are three artifacts for activity 1.B, they can be labeled "1.B.1," "1.B.2," and "1.B.3."

Most objectives and activities are text, but artifacts could be text or image files. Remember to add artifacts to the digital portfolio so that viewers will clearly understand what they are viewing and how it relates to the selected standard, objective, and activity. Because of the need to orient the viewer, the Artifacts section of each standard requires more careful planning and assembly.

The process for adding various types of artifacts to the digital portfolio is as follows:

1. Open the file and select the completed worksheet. Place cursor in the artifact column at the beginning of the designated text. Holding down the left mouse button, scroll and highlight the text to be copied.
2. Left click on Edit and left click on Copy.
3. Open the School Leader digital Portfolio. Left click once on the View icon to make sure file is in Normal View.
3. In the Outline or Slide Screen in the left inset box, select the slide and the chosen standard.
4. Place the cursor immediately after the word Artifacts for the text to be added. Left click once and a gray highlighted box will appear indicating that the selected area of the slide can be edited. Left click the Edit menu and left click on Paste. The typeface will appear much larger. Highlight the text and select 16-point font or other font size in the formatting tool bar above the slide. See the School Leader Sample Portfolio for examples of the result of this process.

Linking the artifact text label to a text or image file or website is accomplished as follows. Left click and highlight the artifact text label that is to be hyperlinked. Right click and select the Hyperlink icon in the scroll bar. In the inset box that appears, select the location of the file in the Look In field. Select the main portfolio project folder. Left click on the selected file (the name of the file will appear in the Address field). Left click OK. Develop a system of labeling and filing artifacts so they can be easily accessed and added to the digital portfolio.

Refer to the ISLLC standard 4, artifact 1.A.1 example in the School Leader Sample Portfolio. Notice that under the icon Introductory Text, text from the ISLLC Worksheet was pasted in the Header Text field, like the process for Objectives and Activities. As a reminder, the artifact is "1.A.1" so it is clear to which objective and activity the artifact is related. Review the School Leader Sample Portfolio (in the Resources folder on the accompanying CD) for other examples of how to add artifacts to the portfolio.

ACCESS AND REVIEW OF THE SAMPLE DIGITAL PORTFOLIO

As previously noted, the CD enclosed with this book includes both the School Leader Portfolio Template and the School Leader Sample Portfolio. Complete the following steps to access the School Leader Sample Portfolio. Place the CD in the CD drive. Left click twice on My Computer, left click twice on the CD drive, and left click twice on the folder titled School Leader Sample Portfolio. Once the PowerPoint file is open, save a copy of the file for your own use as follows: click on the File menu in the menu bar, left click once on Save As, select where the file is to be saved (save the file in the digital portfolio folder referred to previously) in the File name box, rename in the file name field, and left click once on the Save button.

PUBLISHING AND SHARING MY PORTFOLIO

There are many ways to publish and share a digital portfolio created in PowerPoint. We recommend three options. Each option has advantages and disadvantages. First, the digital portfolio can be shared by saving the PowerPoint presentation and artifacts to a CD. There are two types of CDs: CD-RW and CD-R. Assemble the digital portfolio and artifacts by burning files to the CD-RW, which can then be altered. However, the CD-RW is severely limited due to computer software and hardware compatibility issues. Therefore, the CD-RW can be used to assemble but not share the digital portfolio. Once the portfolio is assembled on the hard drive or CD-RW, it can be burned onto a CD-R. The CD-R has fewer hardware and software compatibility issues. However, it also cannot be altered or changed once burned; therefore, it is essential that the digital portfolio be complete, including all artifacts, prior to burning onto a CD-R. A second option is using a mass-storage device. These data-storage devices, plugged into a USB port, are well suited for sharing digital portfolios and have few hardware or software compatibility issues often associated with the CD-RW. A third option is publishing or sharing the digital portfolio to the Internet by uploading the PowerPoint and digital artifacts to a Web page. This is most easily accomplished through the use of FrontPage or some other Web-page authoring software. TaskStream, in the following chapter, is an example of this technique. There are many issues with publishing and sharing a digital portfolio to the Web, including confidentiality of material and fair use.

SUMMARY

In this chapter, PowerPoint was presented as an option to create the standards-based school leader digital portfolio. You received instructions for accessing and using the PowerPoint template and sample completed portfolio on the enclosed CD. Within PowerPoint, you can access the standards-based school leader digital portfolio template; modify the portfolio outline; add objectives, activities, and artifacts; and share the portfolio. You are now prepared to assemble the standards-based digital portfolio in PowerPoint.

ACTIVITY

Complete the formative evaluation rubric (appendix E) at several stages while developing the digital portfolio. Each time you complete the rubric, have a critical friend complete it as well. Compare and contrast these responses. Identify strengths and opportunities for improvement. Develop strategies to address improvement needs. Identify issues and concerns and explore these with a critical friend.

Chapter Five

The TaskStream Option

Chapter 3 culminated in an activity in which you selected one of two preferred digital format options: PowerPoint or TaskStream. Chapter 5 is written specifically for those who select TaskStream as the preferred standards-based digital portfolio tool.

USING TASKSTREAM: THE TOOLS OF ENGAGEMENT

In this chapter, we suggest how TaskStream, an online service, can be used to develop a standards-based digital portfolio. We do not provide training for using TaskStream. After creating your free TaskStream limited account (see the following section), if you have questions about how to use the outline template, refer to the TaskStream Help Index on the website; it includes a vast collection of online and downloadable support materials. To access the Help Index, click the Help Index link located at the top of the left-hand navigation menu (see figure 5.1). You can also click the Downloadable Guides link on the right, then Web Publication, and then the Web Folio Builder download link to obtain a guide to assist you with the creation of a digital portfolio.

ACCESSING THE FREE SUBSCRIPTION TO TASKSTREAM

You receive a free five-month subscription to a limited version of TaskStream when you purchase this book. The free, limited subscription to TaskStream includes access to the school leader standards-based digital

70   *Chapter 5*

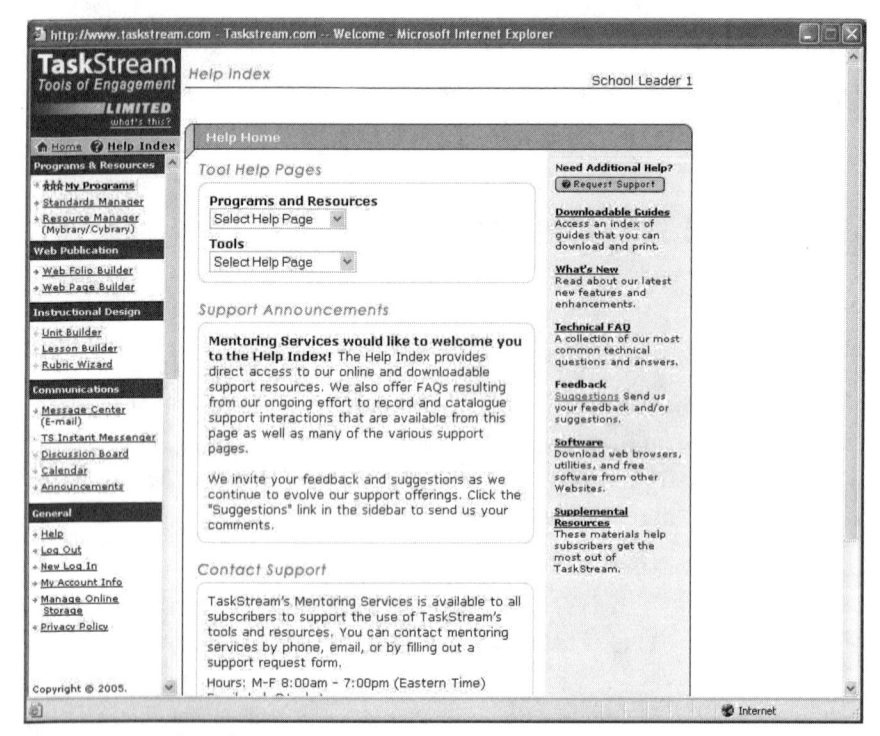

Figure 5.1. Help Index

portfolio template, the school leader standards-based sample portfolio, and other tools. Complete the following steps to set up your limited account. Please note that because the website is frequently revised, the following screens might change. Before beginning, access the CD accompanying the book. In the TaskStream folder is a file, Key Code. Record the key code and keep it handy so you can insert it into the proper form.

1. Go to www.taskstream.com and click the Subscribe Today button on the left part of the login screen. See figure 5.2.
2. Under step 1 you are given a choice to Create, Renew, or Convert My Guest Account. Select Create a new TaskStream subscription. Under option 2 enter the key code from the CD to activate your TaskStream account. Only one subscriber can use the code. Click the Continue button. See figure 5.3.
3. Complete steps 2–4 to finish the registration process.

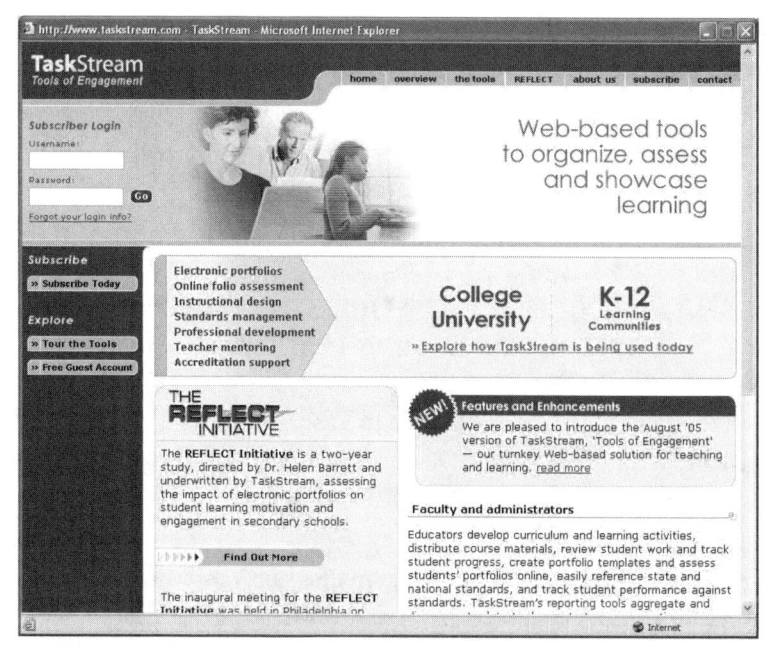

Figure 5.2. Subscribe Today screen

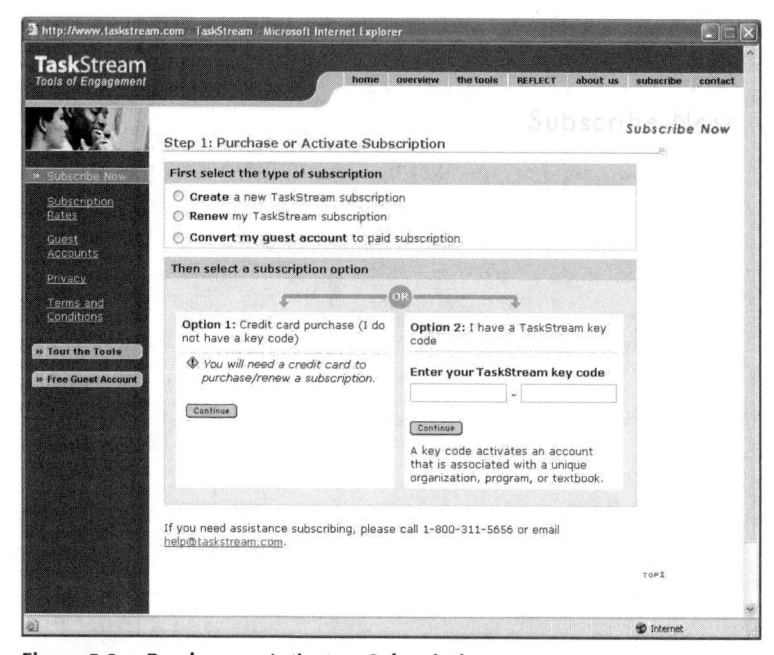

Figure 5.3. Purchase or Activate a Subscription screen

At any time, you can convert your account to a full paid subscription to access the full capabilities of TaskStream. To learn more about what a full subscription offers and to convert your limited account, click the "What's This" link next to the limited logo in the upper, left-hand corner of the site.

ACCESSING THE SCHOOL LEADER STANDARDS-BASED DIGITAL PORTFOLIO TEMPLATE

Along with the free, limited subscription to TaskStream, you are provided with a portfolio template and other tools. Complete the following steps to access the sample template.

1. Log into TaskStream with your username and password. Click the Web Folio Builder link located in the left-hand navigation menu or on the home page. See figure 5.4.
2. Type the name of your digital portfolio under Presentation Portfolios and click the Create It button. See figure 5.5.
3. In step 1, select the template titled School Leader Digital Portfolio Template. Click the Next Step button. See figure 5.6.
4. In step 2, choose a style if you wish to change the look of your portfolio, and click the Next Step button. See figure 5.7.
5. The outline of the standards-based school leader digital portfolio template is visible in the area left of the center of the screen. You can edit the structure of the outline by adding, deleting, moving, or copying a page or section. See figure 5.8.

Log on, click on Web Folio Builder, and select the portfolio you have created using the School Leader Standards-Based Digital Portfolio Template. You can add, delete, move, and copy pages and sections of the portfolio outline using the Edit Structure features in the left frame of the screen below. Note that a page icon is identified as a globe overlapping a page with the top right corner turned down, and a section icon is identified as a small diamond. Scroll down the task bar to the right of the Edit Structure frame and select an area of the portfolio to modify. When selected,

The TaskStream Option 73

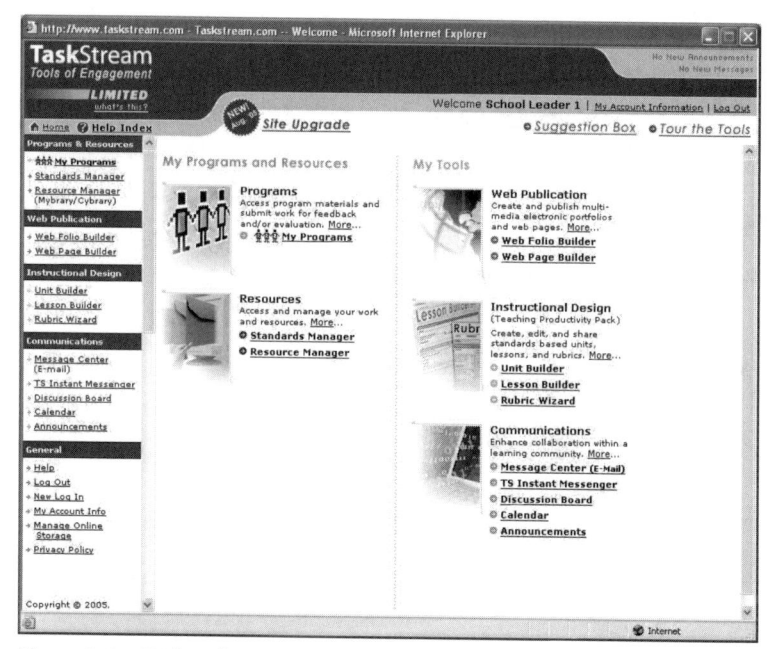

Figure 5.4. Web Folio Builder screen

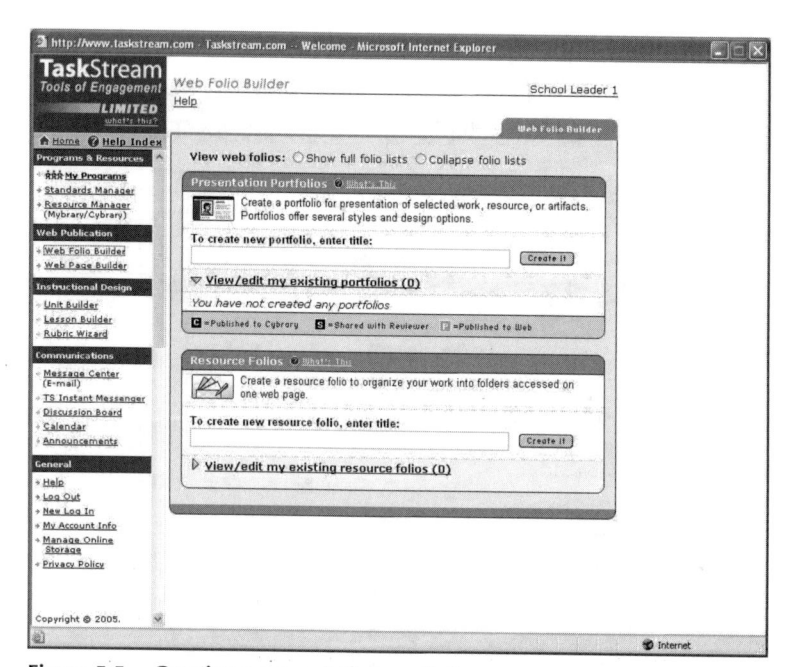

Figure 5.5. Creating a presentation portfolio

74   Chapter 5

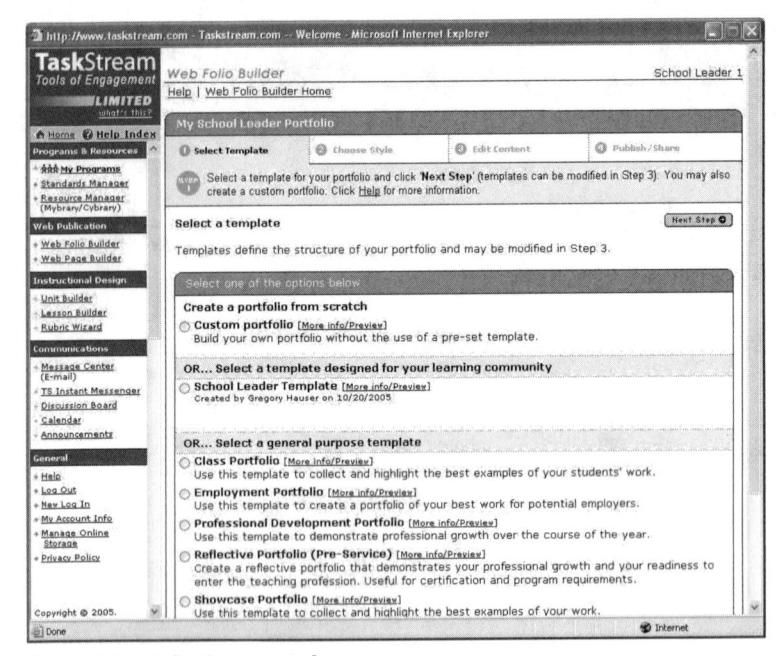

Figure 5.6.   Selecting a template

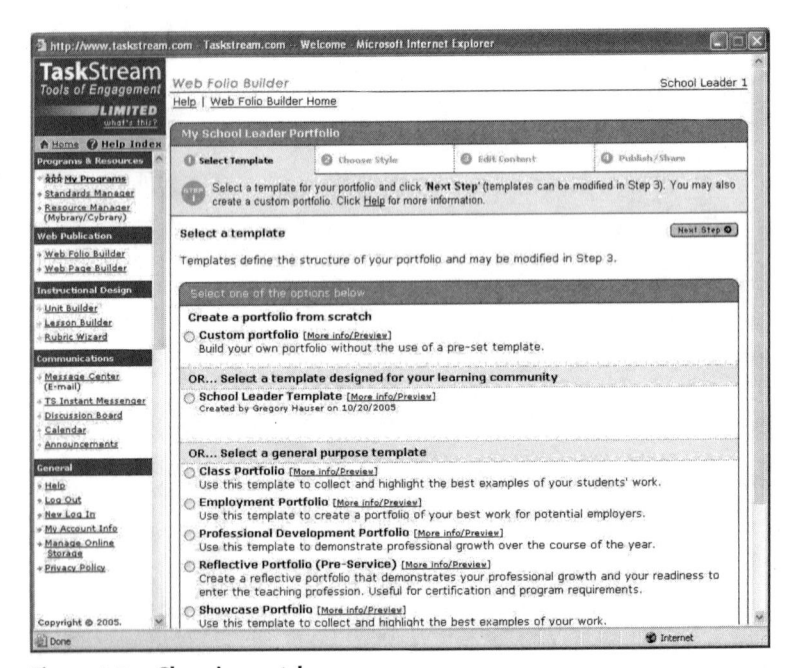

Figure 5.7.   Choosing a style

the page/section icon will change color from black and white to yellow. See figure 5.9.

1. To add a page, click on the page or section of the outline to be modified. Then click the Add Page button from the top of the Edit Structure frame. You can add a page with the options described in the inset box. See figure 5.10.
2. To add a new content section to a page, click on the selected page in the outline and click the Add New Content Section button at the bottom of the right-hand content area frame. You can also edit existing sections by clicking on the Edit button to the right of each section. See figure 5.11.

ADDING OBJECTIVES, ACTIVITIES, AND ARTIFACTS TO THE DIGITAL PORTFOLIO

The central components of portfolios are the documented objectives, activities, and artifacts for each standard. One suggested strategy for constructing the portfolio is provided below. Note that the example objectives, activities, and artifacts for the ISLLC and TSSA standards are included in the School Leader Sample Portfolio on the website.

Prior to adding objectives, activities, and artifacts to the digital portfolio, complete the worksheets in chapter 2. The ISLLC Examples Worksheets file and the TSSA Examples and Worksheets file are located in the Key Artifacts section of the Outline of the School Leader Template. Open and save each of these files under a new file name, either on a diskette, CD, or computer hard drive. For the following illustration, we assume that the ISLLC Examples and Worksheets are saved on the hard drive as My ISLLC Worksheets and the TSSA Examples and Worksheets are saved on the hard drive as My TSSA Worksheets. Once the worksheets are completed (see chapter 2), add the text for the objectives and activities to the School Leader Digital Portfolio. The following three sections describe how to add materials to the Sample Portfolio.

Adding Objectives to the Digital Portfolio

For this task, two programs run simultaneously and you move from one to the other using the buttons on the Task Bar at the bottom of the com-

76   Chapter 5

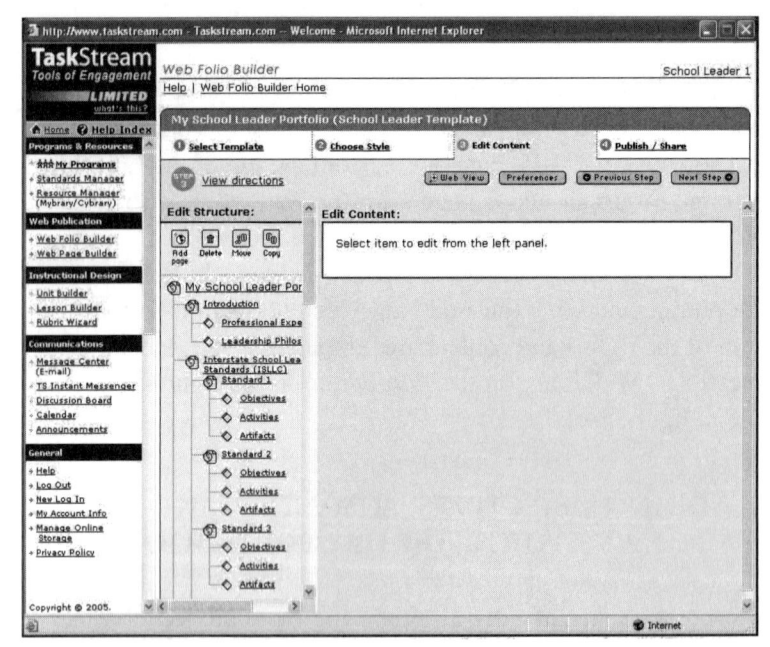

Figure 5.8.   Editing the portfolio template

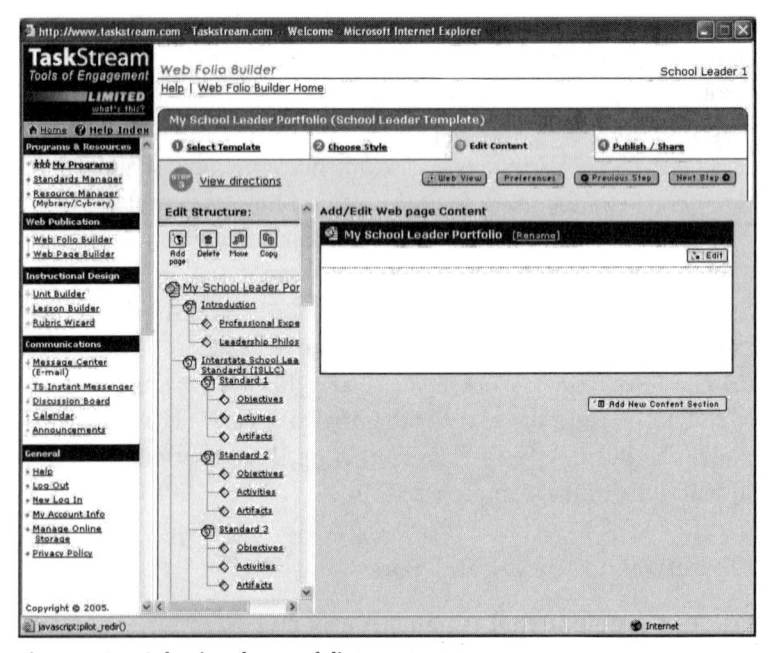

Figure 5.9.   Selecting the portfolio

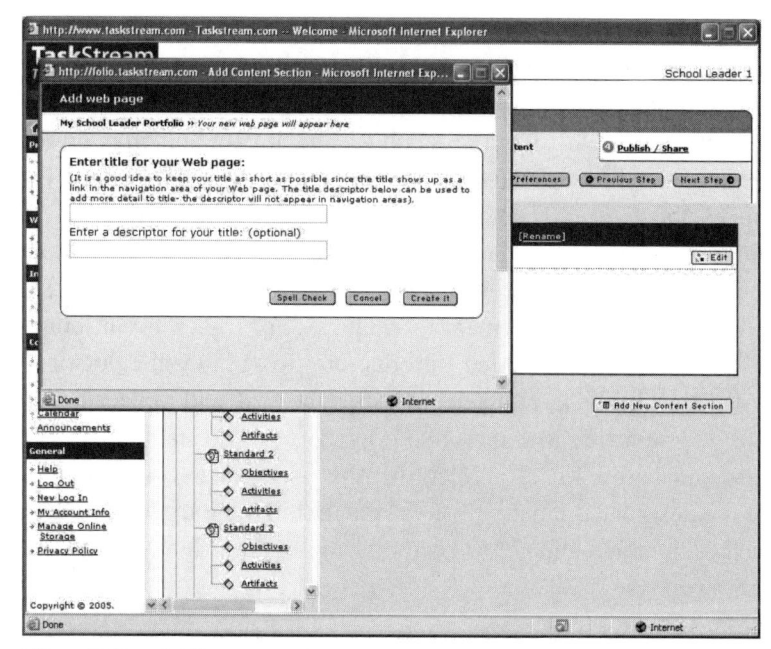

Figure 5.10. Adding a page

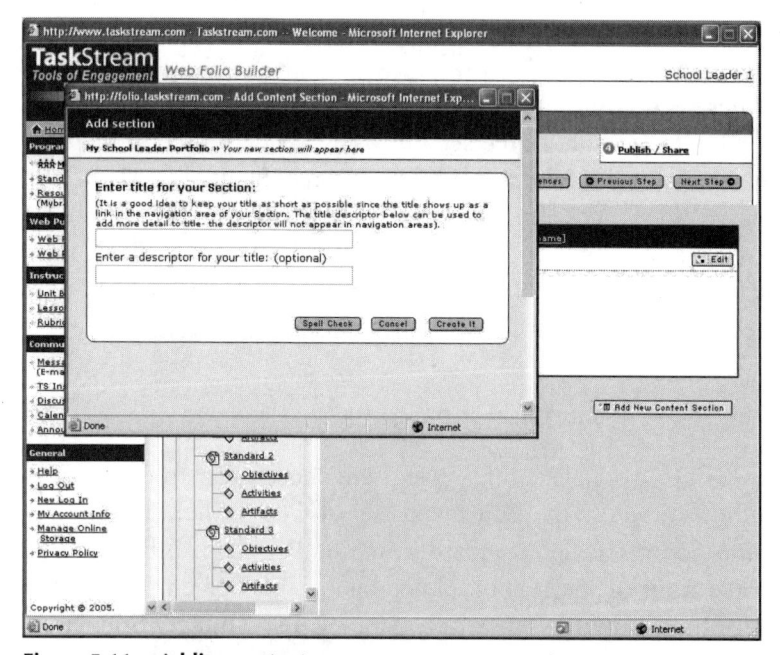

Figure 5.11. Adding content

puter screen. Log on to TaskStream and open your School Leader Digital Portfolio. Then open the completed My ISLLC Worksheets file in your word processor; select the desired text from the Objectives column, and under the Edit menu, select Copy. Switch to TaskStream and click on the Objectives section of the selected standard in the outline field. Click the Edit button to the right of the section. The Content Editor window will appear with the following tabs: Introductory Text, Image, Standards, Main Text, Attachments, Video, and Web Links. Each of these tabs provides a variety of options for adding content to the portfolio. Under the Introductory Text tab is a blank field titled Introductory Text. Place the cursor in the blank field, right click, and select Paste. The text will appear in the box. Again, if you have more than one objective for the standards, code by numbers and letters for clear identification (see chapter 4 for examples). Add the designated label in front of the text in the Introductory Text field and click the Save and Close button at the bottom right of the window. See figure 5.12.

Adding Activities to the Digital Portfolio

Open My ISLLC Worksheets file. Select the required text under the Activities column, and from the Edit menu, select Copy. In TaskStream, click the Activities section of the selected standard in the outline field. Click the Edit button to the right of the section. The Content Editor will appear with the following tabs: Introductory Text, Image, Standards, Main Text, Attachments, Video, and Web Links. Under Introductory Text is a blank field titled Introductory Text. Place the cursor in the blank field, right click, and select Paste. The text will appear in the box. Label the activities so that they are clearly identified with the appropriate objective.

Adding Artifacts to the Digital Portfolio

Open My ISLLC Worksheets file. Select the chosen text from the Artifacts column, and under the Edit menu, select Copy. Click on the Artifacts section of the selected standard in the outline field. Click the Edit button to the right of the section. Once again, the Content Editor will appear with the following tabs: Introductory Text, Image, Standards, Main Text, Attachments, Video, and Web Links. The artifacts section is

The TaskStream Option 79

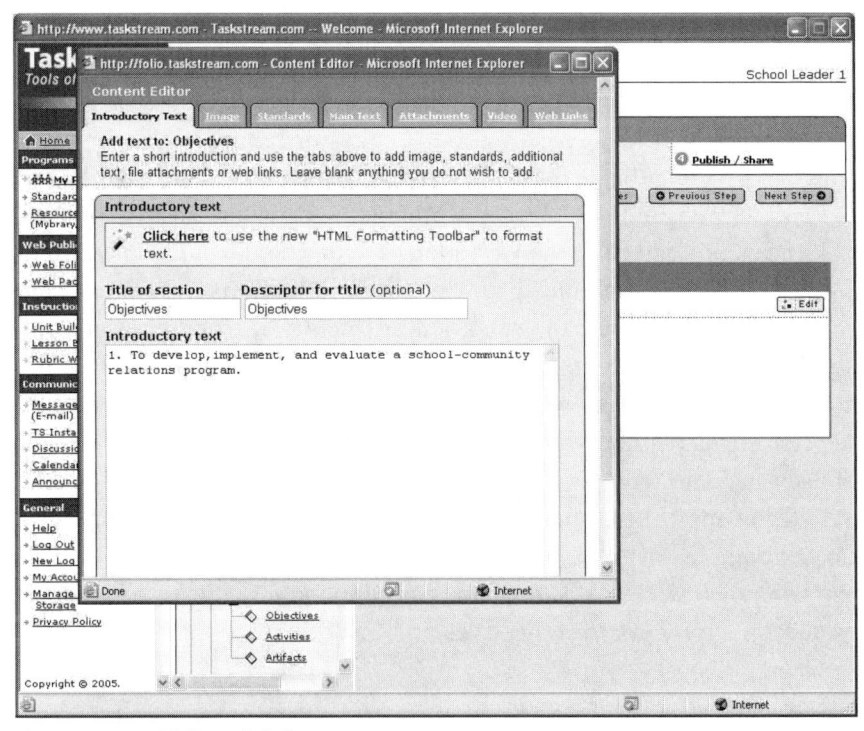

Figure 5.12. Adding a label

more complex than the objectives or activities sections. The various screens for these menu tabs in the artifacts section have different features associated with them. The tab Introductory Text (see fig. 5.13) is a field in which you can insert text. There are also options within this screen for using HTML text. Remember to left click once on the Save and Close Window button after text has been added. You can add images in the Image screen. Select images from the stock images provided in TaskStream or from another source (a hard drive, jump drive, or diskette). Left click once on the Add Image button after you have selected an image. In the Standards screen, you can link other state, national, or local standards to the artifact. The Main Text screen, similar to the Introductory Text screen, is a field in which you can insert regular or HTML text. In the Attachments screen, add different types of digital files such as word documents, spreadsheets, videos, and so forth. For the Name file field, type a brief description of the file. In the Select file field, browse and select the file from a source (hard drive, jump drive, or diskette). For the Describe file field, give a brief description of the file if necessary. Left click once on the Add file button. The Web Links screen permits you to add links from the Internet (e.g., personal homepages or school or district websites). Type a brief name for the link in the Name of link field. In the Link to Outside Website field, insert the Web address. The easiest way to add links is to copy and paste the Web address to this field. For Describe Link, you can add additional information about the link. Left click once on the Add Link button. You can use varied artifacts here, including images, attachments, and Web links. However, artifacts need supplemental information to show viewers what they are viewing and how it relates to the selected standard, objective, and activity. Therefore, the Artifacts section of each standard requires thorough planning and assembly.

Refer to the ISLLC standard 4, artifact 1.A.1 example in the School Leader Sample Portfolio. Notice that under the Introductory Text tab, the text from the ISLLC Worksheet was pasted in the Introductory Text field, by the same process for objectives and activities. Examine the School

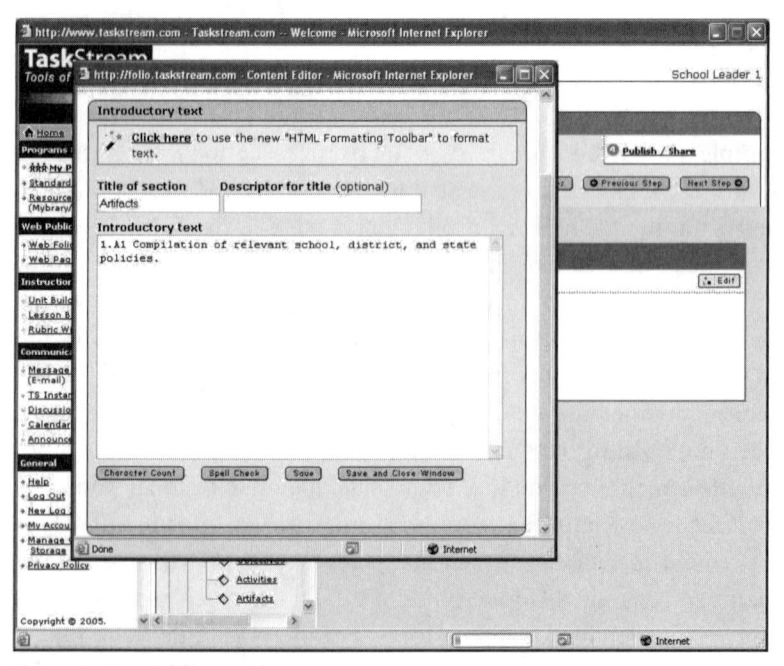

Figure 5.13. Adding artifacts

Leader Sample Portfolio for other examples of how you can add artifacts to a portfolio.

ACCESS AND REVIEW OF THE SAMPLE DIGITAL PORTFOLIO

1. Log into TaskStream with your username and password. Click the Mybrary link in the left hand navigation menu or homepage and then click the Cybrary Shared Resources tab. See figure 5.14.
2. Click [View], on the right, for the School Leader Sample Portfolio. The sample portfolio includes example objectives, activities, and artifacts for ISLLC and TSSA standards from the planning worksheets. See figure 5.15.

SUMMARY

In this chapter, the TaskStream online portfolio option was presented. The process of logging on, registering, and subscribing to TaskStream is a matter of following the screen prompts. Within TaskStream, you can access the standards-based school leader digital portfolio template; modify the portfolio outline; and add objectives, activities, and artifacts. You are now prepared to assemble the standards-based digital portfolio in TaskStream.

ACTIVITY

Complete the formative evaluation rubric (appendix E) at various times during the development process. Each time, have a critical friend complete the rubric as well. Compare and contrast these responses. Identify strengths and opportunities for improvement. Develop strategies for improvement. Identify issues and concerns and explore these with a critical friend.

82   *Chapter 5*

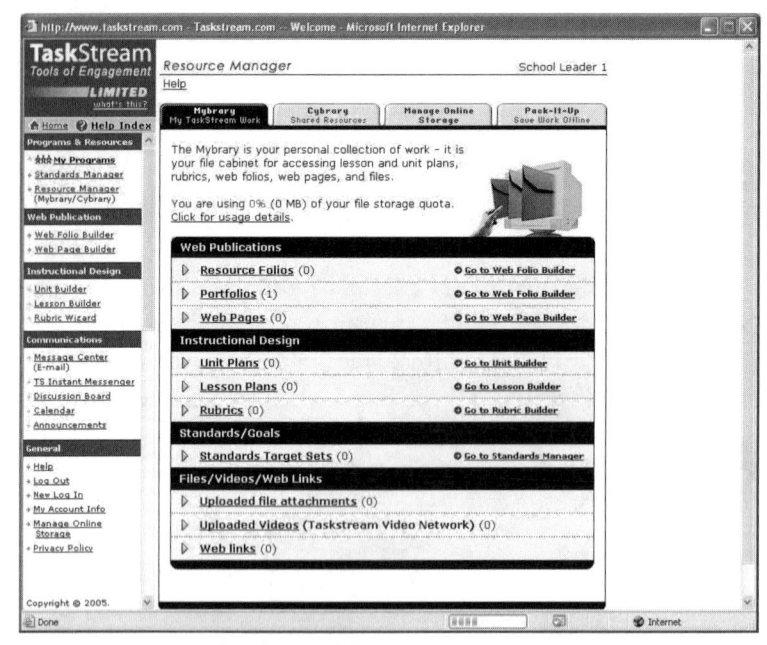

Figure 5.14.   Accessing the portfolio

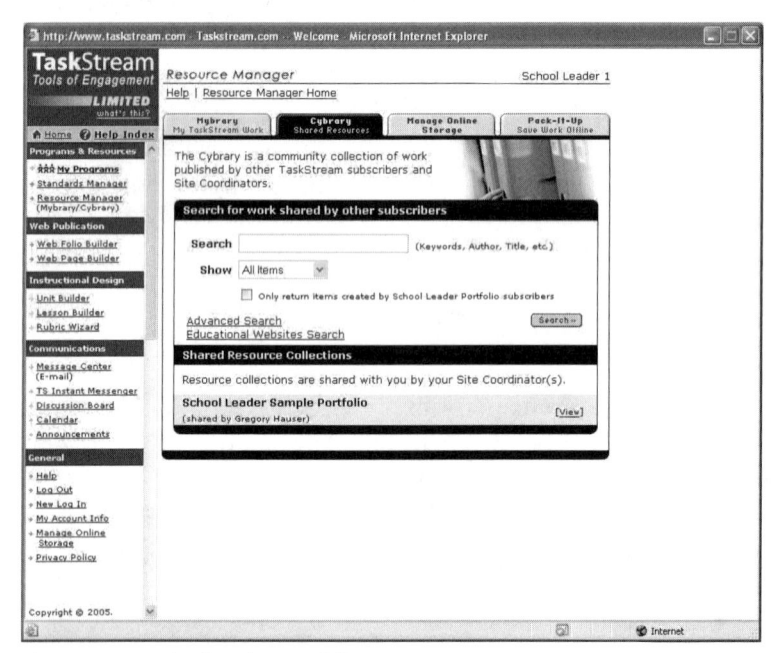

Figure 5.15.   Viewing the portfolio

Chapter Six

Evaluation of the Standards-Based Digital Portfolio

In this chapter we examine why and how the digital portfolio is used to evaluate school leaders and candidates. In this way, leaders and candidates can be prepared to present their portfolios for evaluation. We also include standards-based scoring scales to determine the quality of a digital school leader portfolio.

WHY USE A STANDARDS-BASED DIGITAL PORTFOLIO?

There are four primary reasons that standards-based digital portfolios are useful in evaluating school leader candidates and school leaders. First, school leaders are frustrated with traditional forms of evaluation and need alternatives (Brown & Irby, 2001; Gil, 1998). According to school leaders, traditional evaluations "do not improve performance, do not promote professional growth or school improvement, do not relate to what contributes to principal effectiveness, lack clear definition of job functions, are done to them rather than for or with them, prevent adaptive responses to problems, are oriented to obsolete procedural checklists, are inconsistent and informal, and inhibit open communication and dialogue between evaluators and principals" (Brown & Irby, 2001, p. 5). Not surprisingly, school leader preparation candidates often share these same frustrations with traditional forms of evaluation. In contrast, the digital portfolio offers a more authentic and complete basis for assessing standards-based knowledge, performance, and dispositions of school leader candidates and school leaders. The digital portfolio "not only provides true and rich information for reflecting and assessing the true performance and achievement of learners, but also helps [learners] engage in meaningful learning" (Chang, 2001, p. 145). "Most educators believe that the use of portfolios encourages productive changes in curriculum, instruction, and student learning" (Herman & Winters, 1994, p. 52). Despite these laudable claims there is a lack of empirical research on portfolios (Carney, 2001). In particular, "relatively absent is attention to technical quality, to serious indicators of impact, or to rigorous testing of assumptions" (Herman & Winters, 1994, p. 48). Further, "little is known regarding the capacity of portfolio assessments to support judgments that are valid for large-scale [assessment purposes]" (Novak, Herman & Gearhart as cited in Barrett, 2004, p. 2). Although the digital portfolio is a promising and much-needed alternative to other models of evaluation, further refinement and research is needed to establish the superiority of this assessment approach. We do not address these research concerns; however, the evaluative instrumentation in the appendixes provide a structured framework and a process for evaluation.

Second, school leaders and school leader candidates can demonstrate, through their examples, how to use standards-based digital portfolios both as teaching and evaluative tools. "If principals are planning to advocate the use of digital portfolios with teachers and/or students, they can gain a great deal by participating in the process themselves" (Kilbane & Milman, 2003, p. 144).

Third, because you can distribute standards-based digital portfolios through an e-mail link or the Web, they can facilitate opportunities for feedback and evaluation (Costantino & De Lorenzo, 2002). In sum, the standards-based digital portfolio provides an alternative approach to assessing school leader and school leader candidate competence, to demonstrating leadership by using technology and the portfolio as an assessment tool, and to increasing opportunities for feedback and evaluation.

HOW DO YOU EVALUATE A STANDARDS-BASED DIGITAL PORTFOLIO?

Two common types of evaluation, formative and summative (Scriven, 1991), are appropriate for appraising digital portfolios. The formative evaluation occurs while constructing the standards-based digital portfolio. "The goal of formative evaluation is to determine whether the materials fulfill the intended purpose. The purpose or objectives of the materials are central to this type of evaluation" (Kilbane & Milman, 2003, p. 80). The summative evaluation occurs after completing the standards-based digital portfolio and determines the quality of the portfolio. "Quality is usually measured by how well something compares with a certain set of standards" (Kilbane & Milman, 2003, p. 80).

There are many different types of rubrics available for evaluating standards-based digital portfolios. Some excellent examples were developed by Barrett (2004), Martin-Kniep (1999), and Hartnell-Young and Morriss (1999). The following are eight rubrics for evaluating the standards-based digital school leader portfolio:

- ISLLC self-assessment (perceived importance)
- ISLLC self-assessment (entry skill level)
- ISLLC self-assessment (culminating skill level)
- TSSA self-assessment (perceived importance)
- TSSA self-assessment (entry skill level)
- TSSA self-assessment (culminating skill level)
- Standards-based digital portfolio formative evaluation
- Standards-based digital portfolio summative evaluation

The order in which these evaluation rubrics should be used is outlined in the activities section at the end of this chapter.

There are three scales in the ISLLC self-assessment. In the first scale, rank the relative importance of each element for each standard. In the second scale, identify your perceived entry skill level. Complete these two self-assessments at the beginning of the digital portfolio process. In the third scale, identify your skill level at the end of the digital portfolio project. This self-assessment is applied differently depending on the user. For example, school leaders find their reflection on these scales helpful when creating professional development activities. School leader candidates find their reflection on these scales helpful when developing internship experiences. Because the ISLLC standards are complex, this self-assessment provides focus and a rich source of information for planning and reflection.

Similarly, complete the TSSA technology self-assessment at the beginning and at the end of the development process (see appendix B). Like ISLLC self-assessments, school leaders and school leader candidates apply the TSSA self-assessment differently. With the same three scales, identify your perceived importance of each element of the TSSA standards, your perceived entry skill level at the beginning of the digital portfolio project, and your culminating skill level at the end of the project. The TSSA self-assessment can also be valuable when you have a choice of digital portfolio formats. Use the formative assessment rubric to evaluate your work and share it with a critical friend for feedback (see appendix E). The formative assessment rubric guides reflective assessment while the portfolio is developed. School leaders and school leader candidates benefit from this instrument at various stages when designing the digital portfolio. A supervisor or school leader can use the summative assessment rubric to evaluate a school leader or a school leader candidate's digital portfolio (see appendix F). These are representative samples of appropriate rubrics; however, others could also be utilized.

WHO CONDUCTS THE EVALUATION?

An evaluation of the portfolio may be conducted by the person constructing the portfolio, critical friends, and others, depending on the constituency, content, and purpose of the standards-based portfolio. Revisit chapter 1 for aspects of these three factors. For school leader candidates, evaluations involve the candidate, school leadership preparation members, critical friends, and perhaps site supervisors. Evaluations for school leaders involve the creator, supervisors, peers, and others who can contribute informed feedback.

SUMMARY

This chapter provided an overview of the types, purposes, and methods of evaluation for standards-based digital portfolios. Instrumentation used in evaluating standards-based digital portfolios was introduced for formative and summative purposes.

ACTIVITIES

At the beginning of the digital portfolio process, complete the perceived importance and the entry skill level scales of the ISLLC self-assessment (appendix A). Compare and contrast the responses to these two scales. Give particular attention to those elements considered very important but have the lowest entry skill level. Then complete the perceived importance and the entry skill level scales of the TSSA self-assessment (appendix B). Compare and contrast the responses to these two scales and, again, give particular attention to the elements considered very important with the lowest entry skill level.

During the formation of the digital portfolio, you and a critical friend should repeatedly complete the formative evaluation rubric (appendix E). Compare and contrast these responses. Isolate strengths and weaknesses. Outline strategies to tackle your weak areas.

At the conclusion of the project, fill out the culminating skill level scale of the ISLLC self-assessment (appendix A). Compare and contrast these responses with the responses to the perceived importance and the entry skill level of each element of the standards. Recognize elements that are perceived as areas of strength and elements that present opportunities for continued growth. A supervisor or educational leader can employ the summative assessment rubric to appraise a school leader or a school leader candidate's digital portfolio (see appendix F).

Appendix A

ISLLC Self-Assessment

This instrument provides important information related to your perceived importance of the various standards, your perceived competence at the start of creating the standards-based digital portfolio, and your perceived competence after completing the standards-based digital portfolio. Here is the key for the self-assessment:

Perceived Importance: VI = Very Important, SI = Somewhat Important, SUI = Somewhat Unimportant, VUI = Very Unimportant
Entry Skill Level: VS = Very Skilled, SS = Somewhat Skilled, SU = Somewhat Unskilled, VU = Very Unskilled
Culminating Skill Level: VS = Very Skilled, SS = Somewhat Skilled, SU = Somewhat Unskilled, VU = Very Unskilled

Appendix A

Standard 1. A school administrator is an educational leader who promotes the success of all students by facilitating the development, articulation, implementation, and stewardship of a vision of learning that is shared and supported by the school community.

Perceived Importance					Entry Skill Level				Knowledge—The administrator has knowledge and understanding of:	Culminating Skill Level			
VI	SI	SUI	VUI		VS	SS	SU	VU		VS	SS	SU	VU
									• learning goals in a pluralistic society				
									• the principles of developing and implementing strategic plans				
									• systems theory				
									• information sources, data collection, and data analysis strategies				
									• effective communication				
									• effective consensus-building and negotiation skills				
									Disposition—The administrator believes in, values, and is committed to:				
									• the educability of all				
									• a school vision of high standards of learning				
									• continuous school improvement				
									• the inclusion of all members of the school community				
									• ensuring that students have the knowledge, skills, and values needed to become successful adults				
									• a willingness to continuously examine one's own assumptions, beliefs, and practices				
									• doing the work required for high levels of personal and organization performance				

ISLLC Self-Assessment

Performances—The administrator facilitates processes and engages in activities ensuring that:										
• the vision and mission of the school are effectively communicated to staff, parents, students, and community members										
• the vision and mission are communicated through the use of symbols, ceremonies, stories, and similar activities										
• the core beliefs of the school vision are modeled for all stakeholders										
• the vision is developed with and among stakeholders										
• the contributions of school community members to the realization of the vision are recognized and celebrated										
• progress toward the vision and mission is communicated to all stakeholders										
• the school community is involved in school improvement efforts										
• the vision shapes the educational programs, plans, and activities										
• the vision shapes the educational programs, plans, and actions										
• an implementation plan is developed in which objectives and strategies to achieve the vision and goals are clearly articulated										

- assessment data related to student learning are used to develop the school vision and goals
- relevant demographic data pertaining to students and their families are used in developing the school mission and goals
- barriers to achieving the vision are identified, clarified, and addressed
- needed resources are sought and obtained to support the implementation of the school mission and goals
- existing resources are used in support of the school vision and goals
- the vision, mission, and implementation plans are regularly monitored, evaluated, and revised

Standard 2. A school administrator is an educational leader who promotes the success of all students by **advocating, nurturing, and sustaining a school culture and instructional program conducive to student learning and staff professional growth.**

Perceived Importance				Entry Skill Level				Knowledge—The administrator has knowledge and understanding of:	Culminating Skill Level			
VI	SI	SUI	VUI	VS	SS	SU	VU		VS	SS	SU	VU
								• student growth and development				
								• applied learning theories				
								• applied motivational theories				
								• curriculum design, implementation, evaluation, and refinement				
								• principles of effective instruction				

- measurement, evaluation, and assessment strategies
- diversity and its meaning for educational programs
- adult learning and professional development models
- the change process for systems, organizations, and individuals
- the role of technology in promoting student learning and professional growth
- school cultures

Dispositions—The administrator believes in, values, and is committed to:

- student learning as the fundamental purpose of schooling
- the proposition that all students can learn
- the variety of ways in which students can learn
- lifelong learning for self and others
- professional development as an integral part of school improvement
- the benefits that diversity brings to the school community
- a safe and supportive learning environment
- preparing students to be contributing members of society

Performances—The administrator facilitates processes and engages in activities ensuring that:										
• all individuals are treated with fairness, dignity, and respect										
• professional development promotes a focus on student learning consistent with the school vision and goals										
• students and staff members feel valued and important										
• the responsibilities and contributions of each individual are acknowledged										
• barriers to student learning are identified, clarified, and addressed										
• diversity is considered in developing learning experiences										
• lifelong learning is encouraged and modeled										
• there is a culture of high expectations for self, student, and staff performance										
• technologies are used in teaching and learning										
• student and staff accomplishments are recognized and celebrated										
• multiple opportunities to learn are available to all students										
• the school is organized and aligned for success										

ISLLC Self-Assessment

		Entry Skill Level			
• curricular, cocurricular, and extracurricular programs are designed, implemented, evaluated, and refined					
• curriculum decisions are based on research, expertise of teachers, and the recommendations of learned societies					
• the school culture and climate are assessed on a regular basis					
• a variety of sources of information is used to make decisions					
• student learning is assessed using a variety of techniques					
• multiple sources of information regarding performance are used by staff members and students					
• a variety of supervisory and evaluation models is employed					
• pupil personnel programs are developed to meet the needs of students and their families					

Standard 3. A school administrator is an educational leader who promotes the success of all students by **ensuring management of the organization, operations, and resources for a safe, efficient, and effective learning environment.**

Perceived Importance			Entry Skill Level			Culminating Skill Level		
VI	SI	SUI	VUI	VS	SS	SU	VU	

Knowledge—The administrator has knowledge and understanding of:

	Culminating Skill Level		
	VS	SS	SU	VU

• theories and models of organizations and the principles of organizational development				
• operational procedures at the school and district level				

- principles and issues relating to school safety and security
- human resources management and development
- principles and issues relating to fiscal operations of school management
- principles and issues relating to school facilities and use of space
- legal issues impacting school operations
- current technologies that support management functions

Dispositions—The administrator believes in, values, and is committed to:
- making management decisions to enhance learning and teaching
- taking risks to improve schools
- trusting people and their judgments
- accepting responsibility
- high-quality standards, expectations, and performances
- involving stakeholders in management processes
- a safe environment

Performances—The administrator facilitates processes and engages in activities ensuring that:
- knowledge of learning, teaching, and student development is used to inform management decisions

- operational procedures are designed and managed to maximize opportunities for successful learning
- emerging trends are recognized, studied, and applied as appropriate
- operational plans and procedures to achieve the vision and goals of the school are in place
- collective bargaining and other contractual agreements related to the school are effectively managed
- the school plant, equipment, and support systems operate safely, efficiently, and effectively
- time is managed to maximize attainment of organizational goals
- potential problems and opportunities are identified
- problems are confronted and resolved in a timely manner
- financial, human, and material resources are aligned to the goals of schools
- the school acts entrepreneurally to support continuous improvement
- organizational systems are regularly monitored and modified as needed
- stakeholders are involved in decisions affecting schools

								• responsibility is shared to maximize ownership and accountability				
								• effective problem-framing and problem-solving skills are used				
								• effective conflict resolution skills are used				
								• effective group-process and consensus-building skills are used				
								• effective communication skills are used				
								• there is effective use of technology to manage school operations				
								• fiscal resources of the school are managed responsibly, efficiently, and effectively				
								• a safe, clean, and aesthetically pleasing school environment is created and maintained				
								• human resource functions support the attainment of school goals				
								• confidentiality and privacy of school records are maintained				

Standard 4. A school administrator is an educational leader who promotes the success of all students by **collaborating with families and community members, responding to diverse community interests and needs, and mobilizing community resources.**

Perceived Importance				Entry Skill Level				**Knowledge—The administrator has knowledge and understanding of:**	Culminating Skill Level			
VI	SI	SUI	VUI	VS	SS	SU	VU		VS	SS	SU	VU
								• emerging issues and trends that potentially impact the school community				
								• the conditions and dynamics of the diverse school community				

- community resources
- community relations and marketing strategies and processes
- successful models of school, family, business, community, government, and higher education partnerships

Dispositions—The administrator believes in, values, and is committed to:

- schools operating as an integral part of the larger community
- collaboration and communication with families
- involvement of families and other stakeholders in school decision-making processes
- the proposition that diversity enriches the school
- families as partners in the education of their children
- the proposition that families have the best interests of their children in mind
- resources of the family and community needing to be brought to bear on the education of students
- an informed public

Performances—The administrator facilitates processes and engages in activities ensuring that:

- high visibility, active involvement, and communication with the larger community is a priority
- relationships with community leaders are identified and nurtured
- information about family and community concerns, expectations, and needs is used regularly
- there is outreach to different business, religious, political, and service agencies and organizations
- credence is given to individuals and groups whose values and opinions may conflict
- the school and community serve one another as resources
- available community resources are secured to help the school solve problems and achieve goals
- partnerships are established with area businesses, institutions of higher education, and community groups to strengthen programs and support school goals
- community youth family services are integrated with school programs

ISLLC Self-Assessment

	Perceived Importance			Entry Skill Level				Culminating Skill Level			
	VI	SI	SUI	VUI	VS	SS	SU	VU	VS	SS	SU	VU
• community stakeholders are treated equitably												
• diversity is recognized and valued												
• effective media relations are developed and maintained												
• a comprehensive program of community relations is established												
• public resources and funds are used appropriately and wisely												
• community collaboration is modeled for staff												
• opportunities for staff to develop collaborative skills are provided												

Standard 5. A school administrator is an educational leader who promotes the success of all students by **acting with integrity, fairness, and in an ethical manner.**

	Perceived Importance				Entry Skill Level				Culminating Skill Level			
	VI	SI	SUI	VUI	VS	SS	SU	VU	VS	SS	SU	VU
Knowledge—The administrator has knowledge and understanding of:												
• the purpose of education and the role of leadership in modern society												
• various ethical frameworks and perspectives on ethics												
• the values of the diverse school community												
• professional codes of ethics												
• the philosophy and history of education												
Dispositions—**The administrator believes in, values, and is committed to:**												
• the idea of the common good												

- the principles in the Bill of Rights
- the right of every student to a free, quality education
- bringing ethical principles to the decision-making process
- subordinating own interest to the good of the school community
- accepting the consequences for upholding principles and actions
- using the influence of the office constructively and productively in the service of all students and their families
- development of a caring school community

Performances—The administrator:

- examines personal and professional values
- demonstrates a personal and professional code of ethics
- demonstrates values, beliefs, and attitudes that inspire others to higher levels of performance
- serves as a role model
- accepts responsibility for school operations
- considers the impact of administrative practices on others
- uses the influence of the office to enhance the educational program rather than for personal gain
- treats people fairly, equitably, and with dignity and respect

ISLLC Self-Assessment

- protects the rights and confidentiality of students and staff members
- demonstrates appreciation for and sensitivity to the diversity in the school community
- recognizes and respects the legitimate authority of others
- examines and considers the prevailing values of the diverse school community
- expects that others in the school community will demonstrate integrity and exercise ethical behavior
- opens the school to public scrutiny
- fulfills legal and contractual obligations
- applies laws and procedures fairly, wisely, and considerately

Standard 6. A school administrator is an educational leader who promotes the success of all students by **understanding, responding to, and influencing the larger political, social, economic, legal, and cultural context.**

Perceived Importance				Entry Skill Level				Culminating Skill Level			
VI	SI	SUI	VUI	VS	SS	SU	VU	VS	SS	SU	VU

Knowledge—The administrator has knowledge and understanding of:

- principles of representative governance that undergird the system of American schools
- the role of public education in developing and renewing a democratic society and an economically productive nation
- the law as related to education and schooling
- the political, social, cultural, and economic systems and processes that impact schools

- models and strategies of change and conflict resolution as applied to the larger political, social, cultural and economic contexts of schooling
- global issues and forces affecting teaching and learning
- the dynamics of policy development and advocacy under our democratic political system
- the importance of diversity and equity in a democratic society

Dispositions—The administrator believes in, values, and is committed to:

- education as a key to opportunity and social mobility
- recognizing a variety of ideas, values, and cultures
- importance of a continuing dialogue with other decision makers affecting education
- actively participating in the political and policymaking context in the service of education
- using legal systems to protect student rights and improve student opportunities

				Performances—The administrator facilitates processes and engages in activities ensuring that:				
				• the environment in which schools operate is influenced on behalf of students and their families				
				• communication occurs among the school community concerning trends, issues, and potential changes in the environment in which schools operate				
				• there is ongoing dialogue with representatives of diverse community groups				
				• the school community works within the framework of policies, laws, and regulations enacted by local, state, and federal authorities				
				• public policy is shaped to provide quality education for students				
				• lines of communication are developed with decision makers outside the school community				

Appendix B

TSSA Self-Assessment

School leaders who effectively lead integration of technology typically perform the following tasks. Complete this survey to discover your perceived competency in technology. Your reflection on the responses to this survey will help you determine the format of your standards-based digital portfolio and decide on potential objectives, activities, and artifacts to include in your portfolio. Here are the key terms used with this self-assessment:

Perceived Importance: VI = Very Important, SI = Somewhat Important, SUI = Somewhat Unimportant, VUI = Very Unimportant

Entry Skill Level: VS = Very Skilled, SS = Somewhat Skilled, SU = Somewhat Unskilled, VU = Very Unskilled

Culminating Skill Level: VS = Very Skilled, SS = Somewhat Skilled, SU = Somewhat Unskilled, VU = Very Unskilled

Appendix B

Standard 1. Leadership and Vision: Educational leaders inspire a shared vision for comprehensive integration of technology and foster an environment and culture conducive to the realization of that vision.

Perceived Importance				Entry Skill Level				Educational leaders:	Culminating Skill Level			
VI	SI	SUI	VUI	VS	SS	SU	VU		VS	SS	SU	VU
								A. facilitate development by stakeholders of a vision for technology use and widely communicate that vision				
								B. maintain an inclusive and cohesive process to develop, implement, and monitor a dynamic, long-range, and systemic technology plan to achieve the vision				
								C. foster and nurture a culture of responsible risk taking and advocate policies promoting continuous innovation with technology				
								D. use data in making leadership decisions				
								E. advocate for research-based effective practices in use of technology				
								F. advocate on the state and national levels for policies, programs, and funding opportunities that support implementation of the district technology plan				

Standard 2. Learning and Teaching: Educational leaders ensure that curricular design, instructional strategies, and learning environments integrate appropriate technologies to maximize learning and teaching.

Perceived Importance				Entry Skill Level				Educational leaders:	Culminating Skill Level			
VI	SI	SUI	VUI	VS	SS	SU	VU		VS	SS	SU	VU
								A. identify, use, evaluate, and promote appropriate technologies to enhance and support instruction and standards-based curriculum leading to high levels of student achievement				

TSSA Self-Assessment

Perceived Importance			Entry Skill Level					Culminating Skill Level		
VI	SI	SUI	VUI	VS	SS	SU	VU		VS	SS	SU	VU
								B. facilitate and support collaborative, technology-enriched learning environments conducive to innovation for improved learning				
								C. provide for learner-centered environments that use technology to meet the individual and diverse needs of learners				
								D. facilitate the use of technologies to support and enhance instructional methods that develop higher-level thinking, decision making, and problem-solving skills				
								E. provide for and ensure that faculty and staff take advantage of quality professional learning opportunities for improved learning and teaching with technology				

Standard 3. Productivity and Professional Practice: Educational leaders apply technology to enhance their professional practice and to increase their own productivity and that of others.

Perceived Importance			Entry Skill Level					Culminating Skill Level		
VI	SI	SUI	VUI	VS	SS	SU	VU	**Educational leaders:**	VS	SS	SU	VU
								A. model the routine, intentional, and effective use of technology				
								B. employ technology for communication and collaboration among colleagues, staff, parents, students, and the larger community				
								C. create and participate in learning communities that stimulate, nurture, and support faculty and staff in using technology for improved productivity				
								D. engage in sustained, job-related professional learning using technology resources				

110 Appendix B

E. maintain awareness of emerging technologies and their potential uses in education

F. use technology to advance organizational improvement

Standard 4. Support, Management, and Operations: Educational leaders ensure the integration of technology to support productive systems for learning and administration.

Perceived Importance				Entry Skill Level				Culminating Skill Level			
VI	SI	SUI	VUI	VS	SS	SU	VU	VS	SS	SU	VU

Educational leaders:

A. develop, implement, and monitor policies and guidelines to ensure compatibility of technologies

B. implement and use integrated technology-based management and operations systems

C. allocate financial and human resources to ensure complete and sustained implementation of the technology plan

D. integrate strategic plans, technology plans, and other improvement plans and policies to align efforts and leverage resources

E. implement procedures to drive continuous improvements of technology systems and to support technology replacement cycles

Standard 5. Assessment and Evaluation: Educational leaders use technology to plan and implement comprehensive systems of effective assessment and evaluation.

Perceived Importance				Entry Skill Level				Culminating Skill Level			
VI	SI	SUI	VUI	VS	SS	SU	VU	VS	SS	SU	VU

Educational leaders:

A. use multiple methods to assess and evaluate appropriate uses of technology resources for learning, communication, and productivity

TSSA Self-Assessment

Perceived Importance				Entry Skill Level							Culminating Skill Level			
VI	SI	SUI	VUI		VS	SS	SU	VU				VS	SS	SU	VU
				B. use technology to collect and analyze data, interpret results, and communicate findings to improve instructional practice and student learning											
				C. assess staff knowledge, skills, and performance in using technology and use results to facilitate quality professional development and to inform personnel decisions											
				D. use technology to assess, evaluate, and manage administrative and operational Systems											

Standard 6. Social, Legal, and Ethical Issues: Educational leaders understand the social, legal, and ethical issues related to technology and model responsible decision making related to these issues.

Perceived Importance				Entry Skill Level							Culminating Skill Level			
VI	SI	SUI	VUI		VS	SS	SU	VU	**Educational leaders:**			VS	SS	SU	VU
									A. ensure equity of access to technology resources that enable and empower all learners and educators						
									B. identify, communicate, model, and enforce social, legal, and ethical practices to promote responsible use of technology						
									C. promote and enforce privacy, security, and online safety related to the use of technology						
									D. promote and enforce environmentally-safe and healthy practices in the use of technology						
									E. participate in the development of policies that clearly enforce copyright law and assign ownership of intellectual property developed with district resources						

Appendix C

ISLLC Standards Planner

Appendix C

Standard 1. A school administrator is an educational leader who promotes the success of all students by facilitating the development, articulation, implementation, and stewardship of a vision of learning that is shared and supported by the school community.				
Knowledge—The administrator has knowledge and understanding of:	Priority	Objective	Activity	Artifact
• learning goals in a pluralistic society • the principles of developing and implementing strategic plans • systems theory • information sources, data collection, and data analysis strategies • effective communication • effective consensus-building and negotiation skills				
Disposition—The administrator believes in, values, and is committed to:	Priority	Objective	Activity	Artifact
• the educability of all • a school vision of high standards of learning • continuous school improvement • the inclusion of all members of the school community • ensuring that students have the knowledge, skills, and values needed to become successful adults • a willingness to continuously examine own assumptions, beliefs, and practices • doing the work required for high levels of personal and organization performance				
Performances—The administrator facilitates processes and engages in activities ensuring that:	Priority	Objective	Activity	Artifact
• the vision and mission of the school are effectively communicated to staff, parents, students, and community members • the vision and mission are communicated through the use of symbols, ceremonies, stories, and similar activities • the core beliefs of the school vision are modeled for all stakeholders • the vision is developed with and among stakeholders • the contributions of school community members to the realization of the vision are recognized and celebrated				

- progress toward the vision and mission is communicated to all stakeholders
- the school community is involved in school improvement efforts
- the vision shapes the educational programs, plans, and activities
- an implementation plan is developed in which objectives and strategies to achieve the vision and goals are clearly articulated
- assessment data related to student learning are used to develop the school vision and goals
- relevant demographic data pertaining to students and their families are used in developing the school mission and goals
- barriers to achieving the vision are identified, clarified, and addressed
- needed resources are sought and obtained to support the implementation of the school mission and goals
- existing resources are used in support of the school vision and goals
- the vision, mission, and implementation plans are regularly monitored, evaluated, and revised

Standard 2. A school administrator is an educational leader who promotes the success of all students by **advocating, nurturing, and sustaining a school culture and instructional program conducive to student learning and staff professional growth.**

Knowledge—The administrator has knowledge and understanding of:	Priority	Objective	Activity	Artifact
• student growth and development • applied learning theories • applied motivational theories • curriculum design, implementation, evaluation, and refinement • principles of effective instruction • measurement, evaluation, and assessment strategies • diversity and its meaning for educational programs • adult learning and professional development models • the change process for systems, organizations, and individuals				

Appendix C

	Priority	Objective	Activity	Artifact
• the role of technology in promoting student learning and professional growth • school cultures				
Dispositions—The administrator believes in, values, and is committed to:	Priority	Objective	Activity	Artifact
• student learning as the fundamental purpose of schooling • the proposition that all students can learn • the variety of ways in which students can learn • lifelong learning for self and others • professional development as an integral part of school improvement • the benefits that diversity brings to the school community • a safe and supportive learning environment • preparing students to be contributing members of society				
Performances—The administrator facilitates processes and engages in activities ensuring that:	Priority	Objective	Activity	Artifact
• all individuals are treated with fairness, dignity, and respect • professional development promotes a focus on student learning consistent with the school vision and goals • students and staff feel valued and important • the responsibilities and contributions of each individual are acknowledged • barriers to student learning are identified, clarified, and addressed • diversity is considered in developing learning experiences • lifelong learning is encouraged and modeled • there is a culture of high expectations for self, student, and staff performance • technologies are used in teaching and learning • student and staff accomplishments are recognized and celebrated • multiple opportunities to learn are available to all students • the school is organized and aligned for success				

- curricular, co-curricular, and extra-curricular programs are designed, implemented, evaluated, and refined
- curriculum decisions are based on research, expertise of teachers, and the recommendations of learned societies
- the school culture and climate are assessed on a regular basis
- a variety of sources of information is used to make decisions
- student learning is assessed using a variety of techniques
- multiple sources of information regarding performance are used by staff members and students
- a variety of supervisory and evaluation models is employed
- pupil personnel programs are developed to meet the needs of students and their families

Standard 3. A school administrator is an educational leader who promotes the success of all students by **ensuring management of the organization, operations, and resources for a safe, efficient, and effective learning environment.**

Knowledge—The administrator has knowledge and understanding of:	Priority	Objective	Activity	Artifact
• theories and models of organizations and the principles of organizational development • operational procedures at the school and district level • principles and issues relating to school safety and security • human resources management and development • principles and issues relating to fiscal operations of school management • principles and issues relating to school facilities and use of space • legal issues impacting school operations • current technologies that support management functions				
Dispositions—The administrator believes in, values, and is committed to:	Priority	Objective	Activity	Artifact
• making management decisions to enhance learning and teaching • taking risks to improve schools • trusting people and their judgments • accepting responsibility • high-quality standards, expectations, and performances				

• involving stakeholders in management processes • a safe environment				
Performances—The administrator facilitates processes and engages in activities ensuring that:	Priority	Objective	Activity	Artifact
• knowledge of learning, teaching, and student development is used to inform management decisions • operational procedures are designed and managed to maximize opportunities for successful learning • emerging trends are recognized, studied, and applied as appropriate • operational plans and procedures to achieve the vision and goals of the school are in place • collective bargaining and other contractual agreements related to the school are effectively managed • the school plant, equipment, and support systems operate safely, efficiently, and effectively • time is managed to maximize attainment of organizational goals • potential problems and opportunities are identified • problems are confronted and resolved in a timely manner • financial, human, and material resources are aligned to the goals of schools • the school acts entrepreneurally to support continuous improvement • organizational systems are regularly monitored and modified as needed • stakeholders are involved in decisions affecting schools • responsibility is shared to maximize ownership and accountability • effective problem-framing and problem-solving skills are used • effective conflict-resolution skills are used • effective group-process and consensus-building skills are used • effective communication skills are used				

ISLLC Standards Planner

• there is effective use of technology to manage school operations • fiscal resources of the school are managed responsibly, efficiently, and effectively • a safe, clean, and aesthetically pleasing school environment is created and maintained • human resource functions support the attainment of school goals • confidentiality and privacy of school records are maintained				
Standard 4. A school administrator is an educational leader who promotes the success of all students by **collaborating with families and community members, responding to diverse community interests and needs, and mobilizing community resources.**					
Knowledge—The administrator has knowledge and understanding of:	Priority	Objective	Activity	Artifact
• emerging issues and trends that potentially impact the school community • the conditions and dynamics of the diverse school community • community resources • community relations and marketing strategies and processes • successful models of school, family, business, community, government, and higher education partnerships				
Dispositions—The administrator believes in, values, and is committed to:	Priority	Objective	Activity	Artifact
• schools operating as an integral part of the larger community				
• collaboration and communication with families • involvement of families and other stakeholders in school decision-making processes • the proposition that diversity enriches the school • families as partners in the education of their children • the proposition that families have the best interests of their children in mind • resources of the family and community needing to be brought to bear on the education of students • an informed public				

Performances—The administrator facilitates processes and engages in activities ensuring that:	Priority	Objective	Activity	Artifact
• high visibility, active involvement, and communication with the larger community is a priority				
• relationships with community leaders are identified and nurtured				
• information about family and community concerns, expectations, and needs is used regularly				
• there is outreach to different business, religious, political, and service agencies and organizations				
• credence is given to individuals and groups whose values and opinions may conflict				
• the school and community serve one another as resources				
• available community resources are secured to help the school solve problems and achieve goals				
• partnerships are established with area businesses, institutions of higher education, and community groups to strengthen programs and support school goals				
• community youth family services are integrated with school programs				
• community stakeholders are treated equitably				
• diversity is recognized and valued				
• effective media relations are developed and maintained				
• a comprehensive program of community relations is established				
• public resources and funds are used appropriately and wisely				
• community collaboration is modeled for staff				
• opportunities for staff to develop collaborative skills are provided				

Standard 5. A school administrator is an educational leader who promotes the success of all students by acting with integrity, fairness, and in an ethical manner.

Knowledge—The administrator has knowledge and understanding of:	Priority	Objective	Activity	Artifact
• the purpose of education and the role of leadership in modern society				

• various ethical frameworks and perspectives on ethics • the values of the diverse school community • professional codes of ethics • the philosophy and history of education				
Dispositions—The administrator believes in, values, and is committed to:	Priority	Objective	Activity	Artifact
• the idea of the common good • the principles in the Bill of Rights • the right of every student to a free, quality education • bringing ethical principles to the decision-making process • subordinating own interest to the good of the school community • accepting the consequences for upholding principles and actions • using the influence of the office constructively and productively in the service of all students and their families • developing a caring school community				
Performances—The administrator:	Priority	Objective	Activity	Artifact
• examines personal and professional values • demonstrates a personal and professional code of ethics • demonstrates values, beliefs, and attitudes that inspire others to higher levels of performance • serves as a role model • accepts responsibility for school operations • considers the impact of administrative practices on others • uses the influence of the office to enhance the educational program rather than for personal gain • treats people fairly, equitably, and with dignity and respect • protects the rights and confidentiality of students and staff • demonstrates appreciation for and sensitivity to the diversity in the school community • recognizes and respects the legitimate authority of others • examines and considers the prevailing values of the diverse school community				

• expects that others in the school community will demonstrate integrity and exercise ethical behavior • opens the school to public scrutiny • fulfills legal and contractual obligations • applies laws and procedures fairly, wisely, and considerately				

Standard 6. A school administrator is an educational leader who promotes the success of all students by **understanding, responding to, and influencing the larger political, social, economic, legal, and cultural context**

Knowledge—The administrator has knowledge and understanding of:	Priority	Objective	Activity	Artifact
• principles of representative governance that undergird the system of American schools • the role of public education in developing and renewing a democratic society and an economically productive nation • the law as related to education and schooling • the political, social, cultural, and economic systems and processes that impact schools • models and strategies of change and conflict resolution as applied to the larger political, social, cultural, and economic contexts of schooling • global issues and forces affecting teaching and learning • the dynamics of policy development and advocacy under our democratic political system • the importance of diversity and equity in a democratic society				
Dispositions—The administrator believes in, values, and is committed to:	Priority	Objective	Activity	Artifact
• education as a key to opportunity and social mobility • recognizing a variety of ideas, values, and cultures • importance of a continuing dialogue with other decision makers affecting education • actively participating in the political and policymaking context in the service of education • using legal systems to protect student rights and improve student opportunities				

Performances—The administrator facilitates processes and engages in activities ensuring that:	Priority	Objective	Activity	Artifact
• the environment in which schools operate is influenced on behalf of students and their families				
• communication occurs among the school community concerning trends, issues, and potential changes in the environment in which schools operate				
• there is ongoing dialogue with representatives of diverse community groups				
• the school community works within the framework of policies, laws, and regulations enacted by local, state, and federal authorities				
• public policy is shaped to provide quality education for students				
• lines of communication are developed with decision makers outside the school community				

Appendix D

TSSA Standards Planner

Appendix D

Standard 1. Leadership and Vision: Educational leaders inspire a shared vision for comprehensive integration of technology and foster an environment and culture conducive to the realization of that vision.				
Educational leaders:	Priority	Objective	Activity	Artifact
A. facilitate development by stakeholders of a vision for technology use and widely communicate that vision				
B. maintain an inclusive and cohesive process to develop, implement, and monitor a dynamic, long-range, and systemic technology plan to achieve the vision				
C. foster and nurture a culture of responsible risk taking and advocate policies promoting continuous innovation with technology				
D. use data in making leadership decisions				
E. advocate for research-based effective practices in use of technology				
F. advocate on the state and national levels for policies, programs, and funding opportunities that support implementation of the district technology plan				

Standard 2. Learning and Teaching: Educational leaders ensure that curricular design, instructional strategies, and learning environments integrate appropriate technologies to maximize learning and teaching.				
Educational leaders:	Priority	Objective	Activity	Artifact
A. identify, use, evaluate, and promote appropriate technologies to enhance and support instruction and standards-based curriculum leading to high levels of student achievement				
B. facilitate and support collaborative technology-enriched learning environments conducive to innovation for improved learning				
C. provide for learner-centered environments that use technology to meet the individual and diverse needs of learners				
D. facilitate the use of technologies to support and enhance instructional methods that develop higher-level thinking, decision making, and problem-solving skills				
E. provide for and ensure that faculty and staff take advantage of quality professional learning opportunities for improved learning and teaching with technology				

Standard 3. Productivity and Professional Practice: Educational leaders apply technology to enhance their professional practice and to increase their own productivity and that of others.				
Educational leaders:	Priority	Objective	Activity	Artifact
A. model the routine, intentional, and effective use of technology				
B. employ technology for communication and collaboration among colleagues, staff, parents, students, and the larger community				
C. create and participate in learning communities that stimulate, nurture, and support faculty and staff in using technology for improved productivity				
D. engage in sustained, job-related professional learning using technology resources				
E. maintain awareness of emerging technologies and their potential uses in education				
F. use technology to advance organizational improvement				

TSSA Standards Planner

Standard 4. Support, Management, and Operations: Educational leaders ensure the integration of technology to support productive systems for learning and administration.

Educational leaders:	Priority	Objective	Activity	Artifact
A. develop, implement, and monitor policies and guidelines to ensure compatibility of technologies				
B. implement and use integrated technology-based management and operations systems				
C. allocate financial and human resources to ensure complete and sustained implementation of the technology plan				
D. integrate strategic plans, technology plans, and other improvement plans and policies to align efforts and leverage resources				
E. implement procedures to drive continuous improvements of technology systems and to support technology replacement cycles				

Standard 5. Assessment and Evaluation: Educational leaders use technology to plan and implement comprehensive systems of effective assessment and evaluation.

Educational leaders:	Priority	Objective	Activity	Artifact
A. use multiple methods to assess and evaluate appropriate uses of technology resources for learning, communication, and productivity				
B. use technology to collect and analyze data, interpret results, and communicate findings to improve instructional practice and student learning				
C. assess staff knowledge, skills, and performance in using technology and use results to facilitate quality professional development and to inform personnel decisions				
D. use technology to assess, evaluate, and manage administrative and operational Systems				

Standard 6. Social, Legal, and Ethical Issues: Educational leaders understand the social, legal, and ethical issues related to technology and model responsible decision making related to these issues.

Educational leaders:	Priority	Objective	Activity	Artifact
A. ensure equity of access to technology resources that enable and empower all learners and educators				
B. identify, communicate, model, and enforce social, legal, and ethical practices to promote responsible use of technology				
C. promote and enforce privacy, security, and online safety related to the use of technology				
D. promote and enforce environmentally-safe and healthy practices in the use of technology				
E. participate in the development of policies that clearly enforce copyright law and assign ownership of intellectual property developed with district resources				

Appendix E

Formative Evaluation Rubric

This formative evaluation instrument is to be used by the individual developing the standards-based digital portfolio and by critical friends. The Likert type scale is as follows: E = Exemplary, MS = Meets Standard, DNMS = Does Not Meet Standard, UA = Unable to Assess.

Appendix E

Content Areas	E	MS	DNMS	UA
Consider Planning—Frame and Focus				
How clear is the focus of the portfolio?				
How clear is the framework of the portfolio?				
Is the intended audience identified?				
Comments related to frame and focus				
Consider Collecting, Selecting, and Reflecting				
Do the artifacts match the frame and focus?				
Are the aesthetic considerations consistently applied?				
Are the aesthetics of high quality?				
Are the reflections appropriate and substantive?				
Comments related to collecting, selecting, and reflecting				
Consider Designing, Organizing, and Producing				
Is the content grouped?				
Is the content understood?				
Is the content easy to navigate?				
Is the content organized?				
Do the software programs function?				
Does the software function on various hardware configurations?				
Comments related to designing, organizing, and producing				
Consider Publishing				
Does the portfolio operate in the following media: CD, Web, other?				
How accessible is the portfolio to the intended audience?				
Comments related to publishing				
Other questions or comments				

Appendix F

Summative Rubric

Content Areas	Beginning	Developing	Accomplished
Aesthetic	Few or no graphic elements. No variation in layout or typography. Visually uninteresting.	Some graphic elements and variation in type size, color, and layout.	Appealing graphic elements, layout, type size, and use of color.
Comments:			
Organizational/ Technical	Unclear organization, no or few directions, lack of complexity. Many spelling, grammar, or syntax errors.	Some evidence of organization, some directions, some complexity. Some spelling, grammar, or syntax errors.	Very clear organization, clear directions, very technically complex. No spelling, grammar, or syntax errors.
Comments:			
Focus and Framework	There are few artifacts that address all of the standards, or there are few artifacts that address some of the standards. Most of the artifacts are of inadequate quality.	There are some artifacts that address all of the standards, or there are some artifacts that address some of the standards. Some of the artifacts are high quality.	There are many artifacts that address all of the required standards. All of the artifacts are high quality.
Comments:			

References

Arter, A. (1992). Portfolios in practice: What is a portfolio? Paper presented at the annual meeting of the American Educational Research Association, San Francisco, CA.

Baltimore, M., Hickson, J., George, J. D., & Crutchfield, L. B. (1996). Portfolio assessment: A model for counselor education. *Counselor Education & Supervision, 36*(2), 113–121.

Barnett, B. G. (1995). Portfolio use in educational leadership preparation programs: From theory to practice. *Innovative Higher Education, 19*(3), 197–207.

Barrett, H. C. (1998). Strategic questions: What to consider when planning for electronic portfolios. *Learning & Leading with Technology, 26*(2), 6–13.

Barrett, H. C. (2004a). Electronic portfolios. *Electronic Portfolios: An Encyclopedia.* ABC-CLIO. Retrieved February 8, 2004, from http://electronic portfolios.org/portfolios/encyclopediaentry.htm.

Barrett, H. C. (2004b). The research on portfolios in education. Retrieved March 5, 2004, from http://electronicportfolios.org/ALI/research.html.

Barrett, H. C. (2004c). The electronic portfolio development process. Retrieved January 26, 2004, from http://electronicportfolios.org/portfolios/EPDev Process.html.

Barton, J., & Collins, A. (1993). Portfolios in teacher education. *Journal of Teacher Education, 44*(3), 200–210.

Berryman, L. (2001). Portfolios across the curriculum: Whole school assessment in Kentucky. *English Journal, 90*(6), 76–82.

Bradley, A. (1995, April 31). Teacher board providing valuable lessons in using portfolios. *Education Week, 4*(36), 12–14.

Brown, G., & Irby, B. J. (1997). *The principal portfolio.* Thousand Oaks, CA: Corwin Press.

Brown, G., & Irby, B. J. (2001). *The principal portfolio* (2nd ed.). Thousand Oaks, CA: Sage.

Campbell, D. M., Cignetti, P. B., Melenyzer, B. J., Nettles, D. H., & Wyman, R. M. (2004). *How to develop a professional portfolio: A manual for teachers* (3rd ed.). Boston, MA: Pearson Allyn and Bacon.

Campbell, M. R., & Brummett, V. M. (2002). Professional teaching portfolios: For pros and preservice teachers alike. *Music Educators Journal, 89*(2), 25–32.

Capasso, R. L., & Daresh, J. C. (2001). *The school administrator internship handbook: Leading, mentoring, and participating in the internship program.* Thousand Oaks, CA: Corwin Press.

Carney, J. (2001). Electronic and traditional portfolios as tools for teacher knowledge representation. *Dissertation Abstracts International, 62*(05A), 1798–2065.

Castiglione, L. V. (1996). Portfolio assessment in art education. *Arts Education Policy Review, 97*(4), 2–10.

Chang, C. (2001). Construction and evaluation of a Web-based learning portfolio system: An electronic assessment tool. *Innovations in Education and Teaching International, 38*(2), 144–155.

Chirichello, M. (2001). Collective leadership: Sharing the principalship. *Principal, 81*(1), 46–51.

Cole, K. B., & Struyk, L. R. (1997). Portfolio assessment: Challenges in secondary education. *High School Journal, 80*(4), 261–273.

Conderman, G. (2003). Using portfolios in undergraduate special education teacher education programs. *Preventing School Failure, 47*(3), 106–112.

Constantino, P. M., & De Lorenzo, M. N. (1998). *Developing a professional teaching portfolio: A guide for educators.* College Park: University of Maryland.

Constantino, P. M., & De Lorenzo, M. N. (2002). *Developing a professional teaching portfolio: A guide for success.* Boston, MA: Allyn & Bacon.

Council of Chief State School Officers. (1996). Interstate school leader licensure consortium: Standards for school leaders. Washington, DC: Author. Retrieved February 8, 2004, from www.ccsso.org/isllc.html.

Creighton, T. (2003). *The principal as technology leader.* Thousand Oaks, CA: Corwin.

Crisp, B. L., & Leggett, P. M. (March, 1995). Are portfolios being used in statewide assessment programs? A national study. *Journal of Instructional Psychology, 22*(1), 8–19.

Cruz, J. (1998). Continuous learning. *Thrust for Educational Leadership, 27*(7), 32–25.

Cumming, J. J., & Maxwell, G. S. (1999). Contextualising authentic assessment. *Assessment in Education: Principles, Policy & Practice, 6*(2), 177–195.

Cushman, K. (1999). Educators making portfolios. *Phi Delta Kappan, 80*(6), 744–750.

Daresh, J. C., & Playko, M. A. (1995). Portfolios for principals: Planning for professional development. *Here's How, 14*(1), 1–4.

Davis, A. (2003). Literacy portfolios: Improving assessment, teaching and learning (2nd ed.). *Journal of Adolescent & Adult Literacy, 47*(3), 278–280.

Deitz, M. E. (2001). *Designing the school leader's portfolio.* Arlington Heights, IL: Skylight Professional Development.

Dewey, J. (1933). *How we think: A restatement of the relation of reflective thinking to the educative process.* Boston, MA: D. C. Heath.

Ediger, M. (2001). The school principal: State standards versus creativity. *Journal of Instructional Psychology, 28*(2), 79–84.

Educational Leadership Constituent Council. (2004). National Association of Secondary School Principal's homepage. Retrieved from www.principals.org/CPD/pdf/ELCC_Web.pdf.

Fisher, F. (1993). PEACE. *Journal of Lifelong Learning, 21*, 27–32.

Freire, P. (1973). *Pedagogy of the oppressed.* New York: Seabury Press.

Gibson, D., & Barrett, H. (2003). Directions in electronic portfolio development. *Contemporary Issues in Technology and Teacher Education, 2*(4), Retrieved February 12, 2005, from www.citejournal.org/vol2/iss4/general/article3.cfm.

Gil, L. (1998, October). Principals evaluating peers. *School Administrator, 55*(99), 28–30.

Giroux, H. A. (2001). *Theory and resistance in education: Towards a pedagogy for the opposition.* Westport, CT: Bergin & Garvey.

Hackmann, D. G., Schmitt-Oliver, D. M., & Tracy, J. C. (2002). *The standards-based administrative internship: Putting the ISLLC standards into practice.* Lanham, MD: Scarecrow Press.

Hale, E. L., & Moorman, H. N. (2003). *Preparing school principals: A national perspective on policy and program innovations.* Washington, DC: Institute for Educational Leadership and Edwardsville, IL: Illinois Education Research Council.

Hartnell-Young, E., & Morriss, M. (1999). *Digital professional portfolios for change.* Arlington Heights, IL: Skylight.

Hauser, G. M. (2004). *A constructivist model for creating digital standards-based school leader portfolios.* Proceedings of the ED-MEDIA 2004—World Conference on Educational Multimedia, Hypermedia & Telecommunications, Lugano, Switzerland, 4961–4966.

Hauser, G. M., & Katz, S. (2004). *A case study: Incorporating electronic portfolios into a school leader preparation internship.* Proceedings of the ED-

MEDIA 2004—World Conference on Educational Multimedia, Hypermedia & Telecommunications, Lugano, Switzerland, 2403–2408.
Herman, J., & Winters, L. (1994). Portfolio research: A slim collection. *Educational Leadership, 52*(2), 48–56.
Hunter, A. (1998). The power, production, and promise of portfolios for novice and seasoned teachers. In *Portfolio models: Reflections across the teaching process*. Norwood, MA: Christopher-Gordon Publishers.
Jones, B. F., Valdez, G., Nowakowski, J., & Rasmussen, C. (1999). Plugging in: Choosing and using educational technology. Washington, DC: NEKIA Communications.
Katz, M. S., Noddings, N., & Strike, K. A. (Eds.). (1999). *Justice and caring: The search for common ground in education*. New York: Teachers College Press.
Kilbane, C. R., & Milman, N. B. (2003). *The digital teaching portfolio handbook: A how-to guide for educators*. New York: Allyn & Bacon.
Kimball, M. (2003). *The web portfolio guide: Creating electronic portfolios for the web*. New York: Longman.
Luescher, A. (2002). The professional portfolio as heuristic methodology. *Journal of Technical Writing & Communication, 32*(4), 353–367.
Maeroff, G. (1991). Assessing alternative assessment. *Phi Delta Kappan, 73*(4), 272–281.
Marcoux, J., Brown, G., Irby, B. J., & Lara-Alecio, R. (2003). A case study on the use of portfolios in principal evaluation. Paper presented at the annual meeting of the American Educational Research Association, Chicago, IL.
Martin, G. E., Wright, W. F., & Danzig, A. B. (2003). *School leader internship: Developing, monitoring, and evaluating your leadership experience*. Larchmont, NY: Eye On Education.
Martin-Kniep, G. O. (1999). *Capturing the wisdom of practice*. Washington, DC: ASCD.
Mathers, N. J., Challis, M. C., Howe, A. C., & Field, N. J. (1999). Portfolios in continuing medical education: Effective and efficient? *Medical Education, 33*(7), 521–531.
McDonald, J. P. (1996). *Redesigning school: Lessons for the 21st century*. New York: Jossey-Bass.
Meadows, R. B., & Dyal, A. B. (1999). Implementing portfolio assessment in the development of school administrators: Improving preparation for educational leadership. *Education, 120*(2), 304–314.
Meadows, R. B., Dyal, A. B., & Wright, J. V. (1998). Preparing educational leaders through the use of portfolio assessment: An alternative comprehensive examination. *Journal of Instructional Psychology, 25*(2), 94–100.

Metropolitan Planning Council. (2002). *Education technology: Developing an educational technology agenda for Illinois.* Chicago.

Mick, L. B. (1996). Using portfolios to help elementary education majors gain insight into disabilities and the family system. *Intervention in School & Clinic, 31*(5), 290–297.

Mills, E. (1997). Portfolios: A challenge for technology. *International Journal of Instructional media, 24*(1), 23–30.

Montgomery, K., & Wiley, D. (2004). *Creating e-portfolios using PowerPoint; A guide for educators.* Thousand Oaks, CA: Sage Publications.

Murphy, J. (2003). Reculturing educational leadership: The ISLLC standards ten years out. Paper presented to the National Policy Board for Educational Administration, Reston, VA.

National Commission for Excellence in Education. (1983). *A nation at risk: The imperative for educational reform.* Washington, DC: U.S. Government Printing Office.

National Council for Accreditation of Teacher Education. (2004). Homepage. Retrieved February 18, 2004, from www.ncate.org/standard/programstds.htm.

National Policy Board for Educational Administration. (2002). Advanced standards for educational leadership for principals, superintendents, curriculum directors, and supervisors. Retrieved February 18, 2004, from www.npbea.org/ELCC/ELCCStandards%20_5-02.pdf.

Newmann, F. M., Marks, H. M., & Gamoran, A. (1996). Authentic pedagogy and student performance. *American Journal of Education, 104,* 280–312.

Nicholson, B. L. (2004). *E-portfolios for educational leaders: An ISLLC based framework for self-assessment.* Lanham, MD: ScarecrowEducation.

Niguidula, D. (1997). Picturing performance with digital portfolios. *Educational Leadership, 55*(3), 26–28.

Noddings, N. (1984). *Caring: A feminine approach to ethics and moral education.* Berkeley: University of California Press.

Rhyne-Winkler, M. C., & Wooten, H. R. (1996). The school counselor portfolio: Professional development and accountability. *School Counselor, 44*(2), 146–150.

Richard, A. (2001). Rural schools trying out portfolio assessment. *Education Week, 21*(9), 5.

Rieman, P. L. (2000). *Teaching portfolios: Presenting your professional best.* New York: McGraw-Hill.

Schon, D. A. (1983). *The reflective practitioner: How professionals think in action.* New York: Basic Books.

Scriven, M. (1991). Beyond formative and summative evaluation. In M. W.

McLaughlin & D. C. Phillips (Eds.), *Evaluation and education: At quarter century*. Chicago: University of Chicago Press.

Seldin, P., & Higgerson, M. (2002). *The administrative portfolio: A practical guide to improved administrative performance and personnel decisions*. Bolton, MA: Anker.

Sheingold, K. (1992). Technology and assessment. Paper presented at Technology & School Reform Conference, Dallas, TX.

Snadden, D., & Thomas, M. (1998). The use of portfolio learning in medical education. *Medical Teacher, 20*(3), 192–199.

Snavely, L. L., & Wright, C. A. (2003). Research portfolio use in undergraduate honors education: Assessment tool and model for future work. *Journal of Academic Librarianship, 29*(5), 298–303.

Stanley, C. A. (2001). The faculty development portfolio: A framework for documenting the professional development of faculty developers. *Innovative Higher Education, 26*(1), 23–37.

TaskStream Subscriber's Guide and Portfolio Workbook. (2004). Boston, MA: Allyn & Bacon.

Testerman, J., & Hall, H. D. (2001). The electronic portfolio: A means of preparing leaders for application of technology in education. *Journal of Educational Technology Systems, 37*(1), 3–136.

TSSA Collaborative. (2001). Technology Standards for School Administrators (TSSA). Retrieved July 21, 2004, from http://cnets.iste.org/tssa/pdf/tssa.pdf.

Valli, L. (1997). Listening to other voices: A description of teacher reflection in the United States. *Peabody Journal of Education, 72*(1), 67–88.

Wheeler, P. H. (1993). Using portfolios to assess teacher performance (EREAPA Publication Series No. 93–97). Livermore, CA: EREAPA Associates.

Wiggins, G. P. (1989). A true test: Toward more authentic and equitable assessment. *Phi Delta Kappan, 70*, 703–713.

Wildy, H., & Wallace, J. (1998). Professionalism, portfolios and the development of school leaders. *School Leadership & Management, 18*(1), 123–141.

Wolf, K., & Siu-Runyan, Y. (1996). Portfolio purposes and possibilities. *Journal of Adolescent & Adult Literacy, 40*(1), 30–37.

Wright, V. H., Stallworth, B. J., & Ray, B. (2002). Challenges of electronic portfolios: Student perceptions and experiences. *Journal of Technology and Teacher Education, 10*(1), 49–61.

Yerkes, D. M. (1995). Developing a professional portfolio. *Thrust for educational leadership, 24*(5) 10–14.

Yerkes, D. M., & Guaglianone, C. L. (1998). The administrative portfolio. *Thrust for Educational Leadership, 27*(7), 28–32.

CREDITS

Council of Chief State School Officers. (1996). Interstate School Leaders Licensure Consortium (ISLLC) Standards for School leaders. Washington, DC: Author.

The Interstate School Leaders Licensure Consortium (ISLLC) Standards were developed by the Council of Chief State School Officers and member states. Copyright 1996 by the Council of Chief State School Officers. Reprinted by permission of the Council of Chief State School Officers via the Copyright Clearance Center.

TaskStream "The Tools of Engagement." Copyright 2002–2004. The images of the TaskStream website and all associated marks and copyrights as well as the TaskStream trademark are used with permission from TaskStream, LLC. All rights are reserved.

TSSA Collaborative. (2001). Technology Standards for School Administrators (TSSA). Retrieved July 21, 2004, from http://cnets.iste.org/tssa/pdf/tssa.pdf. These standards are the property of the TSSA Collaborative and may not be altered without written permission. The following notice must accompany reproduction of these standards: "This material was originally produced as a project of the Technology Standards for School Administrators Collaborative." Copyright 2001 by the TSSA Collaborative. Reprinted by permission of the TSSA Collaborative via the Copyright Clearance Center.

About the Authors

Gregory M. Hauser is associate professor and chair of the Department of Educational Leadership at Roosevelt University. He currently teaches the following courses: internship, education foundations, and politics and educational policy. Dr. Hauser's research interests include school reform, technology in education, and comparative education. As an outgrowth of his interest in comparative education he completed a Fulbright Scholarship to Germany. For the past five years, Dr. Hauser has coordinated supplemental academic enrichment activities at six elementary schools and one high school in the Chicago Public School system funded through a GEAR-UP grant from the U.S. Department of Education and two foundations. Prior to his role as a faculty member, he served for seventeen years as chief student affairs officer, most recently as vice provost for student affairs at Roosevelt University. He received a PhD in educational administration from the University of Wisconsin, Madison.

Dennis W. Koutouzos is assistant to the dean at Roosevelt University College of Education. Following a career as a high school English teacher, he served as technology coordinator at the South Cook Educational Service Center and helped design and implement State of Illinois technology initiatives. At Roosevelt University, he redesigned and taught a course for teachers, Technology in the Classroom, planned and implemented the technology lab for the College of Education, and currently serves on university technology committees. Mr. Koutouzos also serves on the Board of Examiners for the National Council for the Accreditation of Teacher Education (NCATE).